FIRE ON THE ALTAR, AUTHORITY IN THE EARTH

Warfare Prayers for Breakthrough, Protection & Spiritual Dominion

"The fire on the altar shall be kept burning; it shall not go out."

— Leviticus 6:12

Donyae Jackson

Fire On The Altar, Authority In The Earth

by Donyae Jackson

Scripture quotations are taken from the King James Version of the Bible unless otherwise noted.

Publisher: Donyae Jackson

ISBN: 979-8-234-00869-5

This book is intended for prayer, devotional, and spiritual growth purposes only. It is not a substitute for professional medical, psychological, or pastoral counseling. Readers are encouraged to seek appropriate professional help when needed.

Table of Contents

The Call to Spiritual Warfare

This book is not written for passive readers, but for engaged believers. Whether you recognize it or not, you are already in a spiritual war—one that targets identity, peace, clarity, and intimacy with God. Spiritual warfare is not just reserved for extreme moments or dramatic encounters; it often unfolds quietly through thought patterns, emotional pressure, distorted truth, and unseen resistance. These prayers are not meant to create fear, but to awaken awareness. When believers understand both the battlefield and their authority in Christ, prayer shifts from survival to strategy.

I did not learn this in theory—I learned it through lived experience.

This spiritual warfare prayer book was birthed from the battles I have faced and the victories God has led me through. My journey has taught me that we are not powerless, nor are we fighting alone. The Word of God is our sword, our strategy, and our strength. Scripture reminds us, "For we wrestle not against flesh and blood, but against principalities, against powers, against the rulers of the darkness of this world, against spiritual wickedness in high places." These battles are real, but so is the authority we walk in through Christ.

The Lord entrusted me with the gift of sight, the ability to see in the spirit. For years I misunderstood this gift. In my spiritual immaturity, I believed something was wrong with me because I could see things others could not, including demonic activity. I carried fear and confusion, not realizing that what God placed in me was not a burden but a weapon.

That changed the day I heard a woman boldly testify about her own ability to see in the spirit. She spoke with confidence about confronting darkness through prayer, commanding demons to flee in the authority of Jesus. What struck me most was that she called it a gift. That one word shifted my entire perspective. I began to understand that God had not cursed me, He had equipped me. He allowed me to see what was coming against me so that I could stand, fight, and win.

"Blessed be the LORD my strength, which teacheth my hands to war, and my fingers to fight." —Psalm 144:1

It is my prayer that this book strengthens your spirit, sharpens your discernment, and empowers you to war from a position of victory, not for victory. Through Christ Jesus, you are already overwhelmingly victorious.

Understanding Your Authority In Christ

For many believers, the struggle isn't believing in God's power, it's knowing how much of that power has been entrusted to us. Many believers try to pray harder when life pushes back. We raise our voices, search for the right words, and wonder why nothing seems to shift. But authority in Christ was never about effort—it was about position. Authority is not something we create; it is something we step into through Christ. When this is misunderstood, prayer can feel exhausting, as though we are trying to convince heaven instead of agreeing with it.

Authority. It is a word often spoken in Christian circles, yet many believers have only scratched the surface of what it truly means. By definition, authority is "the power or right to give orders, make decisions, and enforce obedience." Spiritually, this definition is magnified. Authority in Christ is the supernatural empowerment given by God Himself to every believer. Authority backed not by human rank, experience, or personality, but by the victory of Jesus Christ and the indwelling presence of the Holy Spirit. When you walk in the authority of Christ, you are not standing in your own strength; you are standing in His finished work, His name, and His dominion over all the power of darkness.

Naturally speaking, a judge carries authority because the legal system backs her decisions. Her words carry weight because they are rooted in a higher governmental power. Likewise, a believer's authority is not rooted in personal ability, but in the eternal power of the Kingdom of God. Jesus said, "Behold, I give unto you power to tread on serpents and scorpions, and over all the power of the enemy: and nothing shall by any means hurt you." (Luke 10:19). This is not metaphorical. It is a divine transfer of power.

Paul reinforces this truth when he says, "And ye are complete in Him, which is the head of all principality and power." (Colossians 2:10). To be "complete" in Christ means nothing lacking; no authority missing, no spiritual weapon withheld. And John writes, "Ye are of God, little children, and have overcome them: because greater is He that is in you, than he that is in the world." (1 John 4:4). Your authority flows from the Greater One who lives within you.

This is why God declares, "Not by might, nor by power, but by my Spirit, saith the Lord of hosts." (Zechariah 4:6). Human willpower alone cannot defeat spiritual opposition. But the Spirit of God within you can.

AUTHORITY MUST BE ACTIVATED, NOT ASSUMED

Many believers assume authority automatically works simply because the Bible says they have it. But authority is not passive. It must be acted upon. Scripture teaches that authority is exercised through faith-filled words, standing firm on God's promises, resisting the enemy, and obeying God's instructions. God gives authority, but believers must use it. Jesus did not say the devil would flee because you have authority, He said the devil flees when you resist him.

MISIDENTIFYING THE SOURCE OF THE BATTLE

Another challenge is misidentifying the true source of a struggle. Not every problem is a demon. Some battles are spiritual, but others are the natural consequences of our choices, habits, emotions, and mindsets. Someone may "rebuke" heaviness yet continue to carry unforgiveness, or they may bind a spirit of confusion while not taking responsibility for their own lack of discipline or clarity. Discernment is required to know when to exercise spiritual authority and when to address personal responsibility.

SOMETIMES THE ENEMY IS THE INNER ME

Wisdom teaches us when to confront the enemy and when to confront ourselves. Sometimes the biggest battlefield is not demons; it is our thoughts, our attitudes, our decisions, and the patterns we have allowed to grow unchecked. The "inner me" can become an enemy when the mind is unrenewed or when emotions go unaddressed. Left unchecked, unhealthy thought patterns, pride, fear, unconfessed sin, and self-sabotaging habits will work against the life God intends for us.

This is why Scripture commands believers to take authority not only over spiritual forces but also over their own thoughts. "Casting down imaginations, and every high thing that exalteth itself against the knowledge of God, and bringing into captivity every thought to the obedience of Christ." (2

Corinthians 10:5). This means you have the authority to silence lies, reject limiting beliefs, break toxic inner dialogues, and realign your mind with the truth of God's Word. Taking authority over the "inner me" often looks like intentional repentance, renewing the mind through Scripture, choosing obedience over impulse, and creating spiritual disciplines that reinforce truth in the heart.

Authority in Christ means you confront demons when needed, but you also confront yourself. You cast out what is not of God, and you cast down what God did not place within you. You challenge wrong thinking, uproot fear, silence doubt, and discipline your inner man to come into agreement with Heaven.

WALKING IN YOUR GOD-GIVEN AUTHORITY

To understand your authority in Christ is to recognize that Heaven backs you, the Holy Spirit empowers you, and the Word of God equips you. You are not fighting for victory—you are enforcing the victory already won by Jesus. Your authority is real, active, and powerful. But it becomes most effective when you align it with obedience, discernment, and spiritual maturity.

When believers know where they stand the spirit of fear no longer dictates your response. The fight doesn't disappear, but the way it's fought changes. You are complete in Christ, empowered by His Spirit, and entrusted with His name. Now it is time to walk, speak, stand, and live like it.

SECTION I — FOUNDATIONS OF WARFARE

Know who you are. Know what you carry. Know how to stand.

Before a believer can war effectively, they must know who they are, what they carry, and how God designed them to stand. This section establishes your identity in Christ, your authority, and the spiritual framework that makes warfare fruitful. Here, understanding becomes alignment—and alignment becomes strength.

Knowing Your Identity in Christ

Every battle in spiritual warfare is ultimately a battle over identity. The enemy's first objective is never behavior—it is belief. If he can confuse who you are, he can weaken how you pray, how you resist, and how you stand. This is why Scripture places such emphasis on identity in Christ. Before armor is worn, before prayers are spoken, before resistance is applied, the believer must know who they are and whose they are. Identity is not a secondary doctrine in warfare—it is the foundation.

Many believers do not struggle because they doubt God's existence or power. They struggle because there is a quiet disconnect between who God says they are and how they live each day. That disconnect slowly erodes confidence, peace, and freedom, until the abundant life Jesus promised feels distant and theoretical rather than lived and real.

At the center of this struggle is a subtle but powerful issue: most believers believe their *experience* more than God's *revelation*.

Experience says, *"I still struggle, so I must not really be changed."*

Performance says, *"I'm only valuable when I obey well."*

Pain says, *"What happened to me defines who I am."*

But Scripture tells a different story.

The Word declares, "There is therefore now no condemnation to them which are in Christ Jesus, who walk not after the flesh, but after the Spirit." (Romans 8:1). And again, "Therefore if any man be in Christ, he is a new creature: old things are passed away; behold all things are become new." (2 Corinthians 5:17).

Identity in Christ is not something we earn through obedience or prove through consistency. It is something we receive because we belong. Yet when believers subconsciously believe identity must be maintained through effort, they begin to drift slowly and quietly back into striving. Grace is affirmed with words, but works become the language of the heart.

HOW INSECURITY DISTORTS IDENTITY

Insecurity is not simply low confidence; it is uncertainty about worth and belonging. Spiritually, it often forms through rejection, conditional love, unresolved shame, comparison, or confusing conviction with condemnation.

Scripture says, "For ye have not received the spirit of bondage again to fear; but ye have received the Spirit of adoption, whereby we cry, Abba, Father." (Romans 8:15). Yet insecurity causes believers to live as though adoption is something that could be revoked if they disappoint God.

When insecurity takes root, believers seek validation from people instead of resting in God's declaration. They interpret hardship as evidence of God's displeasure. They read Scripture as a measuring stick they never quite meet, instead of a promise they already stand inside. Insecurity keeps Christians trying to become what God has already declared them to be.

HOW FEAR BLOCKS IDENTITY FORMATION

Fear works hand in hand with insecurity. Fear of rejection leads to people-pleasing instead of obedience. Fear of failure causes believers to avoid calling, growth, and spiritual risk, reinforcing the lie, *If I fail, I lose standing with God.* Fear of exposure traps believers in secrecy, empowering shame to redefine them by what they have done rather than who they are in Christ.

Fear replaces trust in God's faithfulness with an obsession over human limitation. Instead of interpreting experiences through God, believers begin interpreting God through experiences. The result is a faith that feels unstable, anxious, and exhausting.

This tension deepens when believers confuse **justification** and **sanctification**. Many confess with their lips that they are justified, yet live inwardly as though acceptance is postponed until they become better. They say, *"I know I'm saved, but I don't feel accepted."* Identity becomes measured by progress instead of position.

ORPHAN MENATLITY VS. SONSHIP

Scripture contrasts two ways of living. The orphan mentality says, *"I must prove my worth."* Sonship says, *"I belong, therefore I live freely."* Many believers believe in sonship but live like orphans. Fear and insecurity leave identity in Christ understood in theory but rarely embodied in life.

HOW CHURCHES CAN UNINTENTIONALLY REINFORCE INSECURITY

Most churches do not intend to do this. It usually happens when spiritual formation lags behind theology.

A **performance-heavy culture** subtly teaches that faith is measured by how much you serve, how much you give, how quickly you overcome sin, or how "together" you appear. Without realizing it, people internalize the message: *"I am valued when I am useful or strong."* This produces behavior modification, not heart transformation.

An **overemphasis on sin without equal emphasis on identity** also fuels insecurity. Teaching about sin is biblical, but when sin is constantly highlighted and grace is rarely experienced, repentance becomes an act of self-condemnation rather than a return to relationship. God becomes associated with disappointment rather than restoration.

A **testimony culture that skips the process** creates another distortion. When testimonies jump from *"I was broken"* straight to *"now I'm victorious,"* believers who are still wrestling assume something is wrong with them. The slow, faithful work of transformation becomes invisible.

When **leaders model perfection instead of dependence**, hiding weakness and avoiding vulnerability, people learn that honesty is unsafe. Fear thrives where authenticity feels risky.

And when **obedience is taught without safety**, commands produce compliance driven by fear rather than love. Scripture, however, always places belonging before behavior.

MOVING FROM FEAR-BASED FAITH TO SECURE SONSHIP

This shift is not instant; it retrains the heart.

Fear-based faith asks, *"Am I doing enough?"*

Sonship asks, *"Am I trusting enough to rest?"*

Believers grow when they begin identifying fear-based motivation, practicing receiving instead of performing, and reframing failure through the cross. Repentance is not retreating from God—it is turning toward Him.

Scripture reminds us, "There is no fear in love; but perfect love casteth out fear: because fear hath torment." (1 John 4:18). Fear may still speak, but it no longer holds authority.

THE SPIRITUAL BATTLE OVER IDENTITY

Identity is not only psychological—it is spiritual. "For we wrestle not against flesh and blood, but against principalities, against powers, against the rulers of the darkness of this world, against spiritual wickedness in high places." (Ephesians 6:12).

The enemy's strategy has always been to question identity. "And when the tempter came to him, he said, If thou be the Son of God, command that these stones be made bread." (Matthew 4:3). Accusation thrives where insecurity already exists. "For the accuser of our brethren is cast down, which accused them before our God day and night." (Revelation 12:10).

RESTORING CLARITY TO IDENTITY IN CHRIST

Scripture calls believers to renewal: "And be not conformed to this world: but be ye transformed by the renewing of your mind, that ye may prove what is that good, and acceptable, and perfect, will of God." (Romans 12:2). Renewal happens when false identity narratives are replaced with truth until new responses become natural.

Abiding anchors identity. Jesus said, "I am the vine, ye are the branches: He that abideth in me, and I in him, the same bringeth forth much fruit: for without me ye can do nothing." (John 15:5). Abiding trains the heart to experience God as present, not demanding.

Community heals what isolation cannot. "Confess your faults one to another, and pray one for another, that ye may be healed." (James 5:16). Identity is strengthened when trusted people help remind us of what is true during moments when fear and failure try to shake it.

Ultimately, identity is confirmed by the Spirit: "The Spirit itself beareth witness with our spirit, that we are the children of God." (Romans 8:16). When insecurity speaks loudly or fear attempts to redefine us, the Spirit counters those lies by bearing witness to what the Father has already said.

JESUS: IDENTITY BEFORE MISSION

Jesus' life shows the pattern. At His baptism, before ministry, the Father declares, *"This is my beloved Son, in whom I am well pleased."* (Matthew 3:17). Identity is given before it is tested.

In the wilderness, identity is questioned—not created. Jesus resists by truth already internalized. Then, in community, identity is lived, clarified, and sustained.

WHY THIS ORDER MATTERS

Notice the sequence revealed in the life of Jesus: **Beloved Son (identity), Temptation (testing), and Ministry (fruit).** Identity is firmly established before it is tested, and it is tested before it produces lasting fruit.

Many believers unintentionally reverse this order. They begin with service, encounter struggle, and then question their identity when pressure comes. Jesus shows us a different way. He demonstrates that when identity is secured first, pressure can be endured without confusion, and mission can be sustained without burnout. Identity rooted in sonship allows testing to refine rather than redefine us, and it anchors ministry in obedience instead of insecurity.

Identity secured → pressure endured → mission sustained.

The End Goal

The goal is not to constantly remind yourself who you are.

The goal is to live so rooted that fear loses its grip.

Not: *"I must remember who I am."*

But: *"Identity is no longer a question—it is my foundation."*

When identity is settled, the enemy loses his primary advantage. Warfare does not intensify when identity is clear—it weakens. What the enemy cannot deceive, he cannot dominate. Every truth learned here becomes armor for the battles ahead. The gospel doesn't just cleanse you—it claims you. And when identity is rooted, the abundant life of Christ flows freely and without fear.

Understanding the Armor of God

The armor of God was never meant to be symbolic language recited without understanding. It describes a spiritual reality believers are called to live in daily. Warfare does not disappear because armor is worn; it becomes survivable, able to be navigated, and victorious.

There is a quiet assumption many believers carry, often without realizing it—that God will step in and fight every spiritual battle on their behalf while they remain largely uninvolved. It comes from a place of faith, yet it often results in inaction. Scripture paints a different picture. While the victory belongs to God, the call to stand belongs to us. We are not invited to spectate; we are commanded to engage.

Paul writes with urgency and clarity:

"Finally, my brethren, be strong in the Lord, and in the power of his might. Put on the whole armour of God, that ye may be able to stand against the wiles of the devil. For we wrestle not against flesh and blood, but against principalities, against powers, against the rulers of the darkness of this world, against spiritual wickedness in high places."

— Ephesians 6:10–12

THE ARMOR IS NOT RITUAL—IT IS REALITY

The armor of God is often taught as something believers must "put on" through effort, repetition, or ritual prayer. While prayer matters deeply, the armor itself is not manufactured by human discipline. It is already provided in Christ. The armor is not a checklist, it is a spiritual reality that believers live in through identity and obedience.

When believers reduce the armor to a memorized prayer or morning routine, they unknowingly strip it of its power. The armor works only in relationship. Paul does not say, "Be strong in yourself." He says: "Be strong in the Lord, and in the power of his might."(Ephesians 6:10) Strength flows from relationship, not performance. Without abiding in Christ, the armor becomes religious language—spoken, memorized, and recited, yet powerless. Jesus Himself made this clear when He said: "I am the vine, ye are the branches: He that abideth in me, and I in him, the same bringeth forth much fruit: for without me ye can do nothing."(John 15:5) Without intimacy with Christ, the armor becomes religious vocabulary without spiritual authority.

NOT A SOLO MISSION

Spiritual warfare was never meant to be fought alone. Scripture consistently portrays God's people not as isolated warriors, but as a united force—an army moving together in order, covering one another, and advancing with shared purpose. The gospel of peace and the Word of God are meant to be lived out in community, where believers stand shoulder to shoulder rather than scattered and exposed. Isolation dulls discernment and leaves gaps in defense, but unity strengthens resistance and brings stability. Just as an army is most effective when every soldier knows their position and protects the one beside them, the armor of God functions best within the body of Christ. In community, truth is reinforced, accountability keeps believers aligned, and encouragement restores strength when weariness sets in. Alone, believers are vulnerable, but together, they are fortified.

So what does this all mean? The armor functions best where identity, obedience, and relationship remain intact. Lived truth protects far more than memorized language.

Recognizing the Enemy and His Tactics

Spiritual warfare requires awareness, and Scripture consistently calls believers to vigilance rather than fear. Discernment is what allows the believer to recognize what is influencing a situation without becoming consumed by it. The Bible never presents the enemy as something to be feared, but it does warn against spiritual ignorance. Ignorance does not protect—it leaves believers exposed. Resistance often operates quietly, weaving itself into ordinary thoughts, emotional reactions, and even spiritual language. To recognize these tactics is not to magnify darkness, but to remove its cover. Discernment trains the believer to respond with clarity instead of reacting from emotion.

One of the primary reasons believers experience defeat in spiritual warfare is not a lack of faith, but a lack of discernment. When God's truth is unfamiliar and the mind remains closely aligned with the patterns of the world, the enemy is misidentified, the battlefield misunderstood, and the wrong strategies employed. From the very beginning, Satan's greatest weapon has never been power, it has always been deception. Scripture reveals this clearly: "Now the serpent was more subtil than any beast of the field which the LORD God had made" (Genesis 3:1). Deception rarely announces itself as darkness; it disguises itself as reason, familiarity, or even light. "And no marvel; for Satan himself is transformed into an angel of light" (2 Corinthians 11:14). Jesus spoke plainly about the enemy's nature when He said, "Ye are of your father the devil, and the lusts of your father ye will do. He was a murderer from the beginning, and abode not in the truth, because there is no truth in him. When he speaketh a lie, he speaketh of his own: for he is a liar, and the father of it" (John 8:44).

Most believers are not overtaken by obvious or blatant evil. Instead, they are slowly weakened by subtle distortions of truth that go unrecognized. When Scripture is not deeply rooted in the heart, temptation is mislabeled as God's will, conviction is confused with condemnation, and compromise is mistaken for grace. In this confusion, many expend their spiritual energy fighting people rather than discerning powers. Bitterness quietly replaces prayer, offense displaces forgiveness, and division takes the place of unity. Victory is lost when the visible becomes the enemy instead of the unseen. Scripture offers a sober warning: "Lest Satan should get an advantage of us: for we are not ignorant of his devices" (2 Corinthians 2:11). Ignorance in spiritual warfare is not innocence, it is vulnerability. The prophet declared with painful clarity, "My people are destroyed for lack of knowledge" (Hosea 4:6). This knowledge is not merely intellectual or informational; it is formed through intimacy with God and sustained through obedience to His Word.

IDENTITY HAS ALWAYS BEEN THE TARGET

Long before behavior is challenged, identity is questioned. This has always been the enemy's strategy. In the wilderness, Satan did not begin by tempting Jesus with sin—he began by probing His sonship. The temptation was not about hunger; it was about identity. In the same way, believers lose ground when they forget who they are in Christ, when emotions become louder than truth, or when circumstances are allowed to define reality. Scripture reveals the weight of this inner battle: "For as he thinketh in his heart, so is he" (Proverbs 23:7). What is believed internally will eventually be lived externally.

ISOLATION WEAKENS THE BATTLE LINE

God never intended spiritual warfare to be fought alone. Scripture consistently affirms the power of unity, reminding us, "Two are better than one; because they have a good reward for their labour. For if they fall, the one will lift up his fellow: but woe to him that is alone when he falleth; for he hath not another to help him up... and a threefold cord is not quickly broken" (Ecclesiastes 4:9–12). Isolation does not make believers stronger; it makes them vulnerable. The enemy understands this well, which is why Scripture warns, "Be sober, be vigilant; because your adversary the devil, as a roaring lion, walketh about, seeking whom he may devour" (1 Peter 5:8). Lions do not attack the herd, they target the one who strays.

AUTHORITY BEGINS WITH ALIGNMENT

Spiritual authority does not originate in confrontation; it flows from surrender. Scripture gives the order clearly and without ambiguity: "Submit yourselves therefore to God. Resist the devil, and he will flee from you" (James 4:7). Many attempt resistance without submission and are left frustrated, exhausted, and confused. Authority is not released through intensity or repetition; it flows from alignment with God's will and obedience to His Word.

MODERN DECEPTIONS THAT WEAKEN THE CHURCH

Some of the most destructive deceptions in the Church today sound spiritual, yet quietly strip believers of spiritual authority. One of the most subtle deceptions is grace preached without repentance. Paul confronts this distortion directly: "What shall we say then? Shall we continue in sin, that grace may abound? God forbid" (Romans 6:1–2). True grace never excuses compromise, it empowers transformation. Scripture affirms this clearly: "For the grace of God that bringeth salvation hath appeared to all men, teaching us that, denying ungodliness and worldly lusts, we should live soberly, righteously, and godly, in this present world" (Titus 2:11–12).

Another deception emerges when emotional experience replaces biblical truth. Feelings are real, but they are not reliable guides. Scripture cautions us soberly, "The heart is deceitful above all things, and desperately wicked: who can know it?" (Jeremiah 17:9). For this reason, believers are instructed, "Beloved, believe not every spirit, but try the spirits whether they are of God" (1 John 4:1). Discernment must be anchored in truth, not emotional reaction.

A gospel stripped of the cross produces disciples unprepared for pressure. Jesus set the standard without hesitation when He said, "If any man will come after me, let him deny himself, and take up his cross daily, and follow me" (Luke 9:23). Victory without surrender leaves believers spiritually underdeveloped and easily deceived.

HOW DISCERNMENT IS FORMED

Discernment is not automatic; it is trained through consistent obedience and practice. Scripture explains, "But strong meat belongeth to them that are of full age, even those who by reason of use have their senses exercised to discern both good and evil" (Hebrews 5:14). Discernment matures as believers immerse themselves in Scripture, walk honestly in the light, obey revealed truth, and remain accountable within godly community.

JESUS: THE MODEL OF SPIRITUAL CLARITY

Jesus modeled this perfectly. In the wilderness, He did not negotiate with emotion, reason with circumstance, or debate logic. He responded with truth rightly applied, declaring, "It is written" (Matthew 4:4). His authority flowed not from self-assertion but from union with the Father. As He said plainly, "The Son can do nothing of himself, but what he seeth the Father do: for what things soever he doeth, these also doeth the Son likewise" (John 5:19). Alignment preceded authority.

A FINAL WARNING—AND A GREATER ASSURANCE

Scripture offers both a sobering warning and a steady hope. "For the time will come when they will not endure sound doctrine; but after their own lusts shall they heap to themselves teachers, having itching ears" (2 Timothy 4:3). Yet believers are not left powerless or unprotected. "But ye have an unction from the Holy One, and ye know all things" (1 John 2:20). Discernment remains available to those who love truth more than comfort, submission more than self, and Christ more than convenience. Believers who stay anchored in truth are never as vulnerable as deception would suggest.

Discernment not only reveals the enemy's tactics—it calls you to examine where the enemy finds room to operate.

Recognizing the enemy's tactics is only the beginning of discernment. Once you understand *who* you are contending with, the next question naturally follows: *How does the enemy gain influence in the first place?* Without clarity here, you may pray fervently yet feel stuck, rebuking what should be repented of, or resisting what requires healing. Scripture teaches that victory is not only about confronting the enemy, but about closing the places where he attempts to operate. This requires honesty, wisdom, and a willingness to let God search the heart.

UNDERSTANDING ACCESS POINTS OF THE ENEMY

Not every spiritual battle begins the same way. Some resistance comes suddenly, while other struggles linger quietly for years. Without discernment, believers can either over-spiritualize every difficulty or ignore genuine spiritual interference altogether. Scripture makes it clear that while the enemy is defeated, he still looks for opportunity. Awareness of how access occurs is not meant to produce fear—it is meant to restore clarity and authority.

The Bible reminds us that "neither give place to the devil" (Ephesians 4:27). That instruction alone tells us something important: access is not automatic. It is permitted, opened, or tolerated—sometimes knowingly, often unknowingly. Understanding access points helps believers stop fighting blindly and begin responding wisely.

One common access point is **unresolved sin or disobedience**. This does not mean that every struggle is the result of personal failure, nor does it imply that believers lose their salvation when they stumble. But Scripture consistently teaches that unrepented sin dulls spiritual discernment and weakens resistance. When areas of life remain unsubmitted to God, the enemy exploits the gap—not because he has authority, but because alignment has been compromised. James writes, "Submit yourselves therefore to God. Resist the devil, and he will flee from you" (James 4:7). Submission comes before resistance. Authority flows from alignment.

Another access point is **wounds that were never healed**—places where pain, trauma, rejection, or abuse shaped internal beliefs. The enemy often builds strongholds not through dramatic encounters, but through lies quietly planted in moments of vulnerability. Paul speaks directly to this inner battleground when he writes, "Casting down imaginations, and every high thing that exalteth itself against the knowledge of God, and bringing into captivity every thought to the obedience of Christ" (2 Corinthians 10:5). When lies are left unchallenged, they become places the enemy revisits. Healing and truth close doors that prayer alone cannot.

There is also the matter of **covenants and agreements**, a topic often misunderstood or avoided. Not all covenants are dramatic or occult. Many are subtle—spoken words, internal vows, generational patterns, or agreements made in moments of fear, grief, or desperation. Statements like *"I'll always be alone," "I'll never trust again,"* or *"This is just who I am"* can become internal agreements that shape behavior and expectation. Scripture warns us that "death and life are in the power of the tongue" (Proverbs 18:21). What is spoken repeatedly can become spiritually reinforced.

At the same time, Scripture does not shy away from acknowledging **occultic practices**—divination, witchcraft, sorcery, and other spiritual activities that seek power apart from God. These practices are not imaginary, nor are they harmless. They represent counterfeit authority and spiritual contracts outside the lordship of Christ. God's warning in Scripture is not rooted in fear, but protection. "There shall not be found among you any one that maketh his son or his daughter to pass through the fire, or that useth divination, or an observer of times, or an enchanter, or a witch" (Deuteronomy 18:10). The purpose of this knowledge is not to make you anxious, but informed. Ignorance does not protect—it exposes. As the Lord declares, "My people are destroyed for lack of knowledge" (Hosea 4:6).

Another often-overlooked access point is **calling and assignment**. Scripture shows us that resistance frequently intensifies where purpose is present. The enemy does not attack what poses no threat. From the moment Jesus was publicly affirmed—"This is my beloved Son, in whom I am well pleased" (Matthew 3:17)—He was led into the wilderness to be tempted. The attack was not random; it was targeted. In the same way, believers who are growing, maturing, or stepping into greater obedience may experience increased resistance—not because they are failing, but because they are advancing.

Understanding access points does not mean obsessing over darkness. It means recognizing patterns so they can be addressed through truth, repentance, healing, and authority. Not every battle requires rebuke; some require repentance. Not every struggle is demonic; some are emotional, relational, or rooted in the flesh. Wisdom discerns the difference.

When access is closed, authority becomes effective. The enemy's foothold is broken not by self-effort, but through alignment. The believer who understands where battles originate can pray with clarity, resist with confidence, and walk forward without fear. This is not about seeing an enemy everywhere; it is about ensuring there is no place left for him to stand. With the enemy identified, you can now learn how to stand from victory rather than fight to obtain it.

How to Pray from Victory, Not for Victory

Prayer reveals posture. Whether a believer prays from victory or for it determines how warfare is experienced. Prayer was never meant to secure what Christ has already accomplished, it was designed to enforce it.

Many believers pray as if victory is still up in the air—like God needs extra convincing to step in. The prayers are heartfelt and intense, sometimes even desperate, but underneath them is an unspoken belief: *I'm still trying to get something I don't really have yet.* This "fight for victory" mindset usually isn't about rebellion or lack of faith. It's more often the result of feeling disconnected—from God's nearness, from peace, or from the reality that the work Christ finished was already enough.

When someone believes they're still trying to secure victory with God, everything starts to feel draining. Spiritual resistance feels heavy instead of hopeful. Emotional struggles feel like personal failures. Prayer turns into work instead of rest. This usually happens when identity in Christ hasn't fully settled in the heart. Even though Jesus' death and resurrection already defeated sin, death, and the power of the enemy, many believers still live as if victory depends on their effort, consistency, or spiritual intensity. In spaces where striving is emphasized more than grace, it's easy to start believing that peace, breakthrough, or God's approval has to be fought for instead of received. Over time, prayer shifts from agreement with God to trying to win something He already gave.

Yet Scripture tells a different story. There is another way to stand in the middle of the battle—one that doesn't ignore the reality of warfare, but changes how we face it. This is the posture of those who understand they are not fighting *for* victory, but *from* it. They know that Christ has already overcome the enemy, and they are standing inside that finished triumph. Their prayers are not reaching for victory as if it's far away; they are enforcing what has already been secured. As Paul writes, "Nay, in all these things we are more than conquerors through him that loved us" (Romans 8:37). And again he reminds us, "But thanks be to God, which giveth us the victory through our Lord Jesus Christ" (1 Corinthians 15:57). This perspective doesn't deny hardship—it reframes it. You are no longer a victim begging for relief, but a son or daughter standing firmly in what has already been given.

Whether someone lives from victory or continues to fight for it is often shaped by what they've walked through. Long seasons of struggle—mental, emotional, relational, or spiritual can slowly train the heart to expect opposition instead of rest. After a while, suffering can cloud how you see things, so victory starts to feel distant instead of present. Church culture can reinforce this as well. Scripture does call us to resist sin and stand firm, but when everything is framed as a constant battle and not enough time is spent anchoring us in what Christ has already finished, people don't walk away stronger—they walk away exhausted.

The enemy knows how to take advantage of this weakness. Scripture calls Satan "the accuser of the brethren," and his aim is always the same—to convince believers that they have something to prove or a place to earn. Where identity is shaky, doubt finds room to grow. When a believer begins to question their worth, God's promises start to feel farther away, and prayer slowly shifts from quiet confidence to anxious pleading.

The way forward begins with truth. Praying from victory doesn't start with a list of requests—it starts with remembering what God has already said. Before asking God to move, align your heart with what God has already said. *Father, thank You that I am accepted in Christ. Thank You that sin no longer has dominion over me. Thank You that You have given me wisdom, strength, and self-control.* This posture re-centers the soul not in lack, but in inheritance.

When Scripture is prayed this way, it becomes agreement rather than negotiation. Instead of saying, *Lord, help me believe Your Word,* the prayer shifts to, *Lord, Your Word says this is true, and I choose to stand with it—even when my feelings push back.* Faith isn't pretending nothing hurts; it's choosing alignment over emotion. And praying from victory doesn't mean becoming independent from God. It isn't self-confidence—it's trust in God. It says, *Because You have already won, I don't have to carry this alone. I can walk it out with You.*

From this place, obedience becomes the evidence of belief. After reading Scripture, the most powerful question is often the simplest one: *What does this change about how I live today?* Who must be forgiven? What thought must be challenged? What reaction must be surrendered? Victory isn't proven by how we feel in the moment—it's revealed by sustained obedience.

Jesus Himself taught that fruitfulness flows from abiding, not self-effort. "I am the vine, ye are the branches: He that abideth in me, and I in him, the same bringeth forth much fruit: for without me ye can do nothing" (John 15:5). Time spent in God's presence has a way of putting life back into proper order. It reminds you who you are, quiets the fears that creep in, and brings clarity where confusion has settled. Victory isn't something you have to activate through effort; it's something you remain connected to through relationship. And when that connection is neglected, you can feel it. You begin leaning on your own reasoning instead of trusting God. Emotions start leading instead of discernment. Other voices—opinions, fears, pressure—grow louder than the voice of God.

Discernment develops the same way—slowly, over time, through consistency rather than intensity. Scripture says, "But strong meat belongeth to them that are of full age, even those who by reason of use have their senses exercised to discern both good and evil" (Hebrews 5:14). Regular time in the Word trains your spiritual instincts. It helps you recognize God's character, notice when something feels off, and test spiritual language against unchanging truth. Without that grounding, even sincere believers can be drawn in by charisma, emotional highs, or things that *sound* spiritual. Scripture gives this sober reminder: "And no marvel; for Satan himself is transformed into an angel of light" (2 Corinthians 11:14).

True discernment does not leave you suspicious or anxious. Suspicion often pretends to be wisdom, but it breeds fear, accusation, and division. Discernment, on the other hand, draws the heart closer to Jesus. Jesus said plainly, "Ye shall know them by their fruits" (Matthew 7:16, KJV). Fruit reveals what language can conceal —humility, repentance, submission to Scripture, love, and steady faithfulness. Deception can sound convincing for a season, but it cannot sustain godly fruit in the long run

Scripture does not portray believers as fragile targets constantly at risk of being overtaken. It presents you as seated with Christ, sealed by the Spirit, and strengthened through relationship with Him. "Greater is he that is in you, than he that is in the world" (1 John 4:4). Darkness does not overpower those who walk in the light; light exposes darkness naturally. The enemy is not overcome by obsessing over darkness, but by growing in revelation of Christ.

Victory, then, is not maintained by watching the enemy—it is maintained by staying close to Jesus. Peter writes, "Be sober, be vigilant; because your adversary the devil, as a roaring lion, walketh about, seeking whom he may devour: Whom resist stedfast in the faith" (1 Peter 5:8–9). When your attention stays fixed on threats, schemes, or what *might* happen, it's easy to forget where your true strength lies. Peace and steadiness flow from remaining rooted in Christ, not from just constantly monitoring the enemy.

At the root of praying *for* victory instead of *from* victory is identity. Prayer changes depending on how we see ourselves. When we feel powerless, we beg. When we feel uncertain, we struggle to push through. When we feel defeated, we plead. But when we know who we are in Christ—prayer simply becomes speaking in agreement with what God has already done. To pray from victory is to stand on what God has already declared, to enforce truth rather than ask God to repeat what He has already accomplished. It is the difference between saying, *God, please give me peace*, and praying, *God, You said You are my peace—help me walk in that today.*

When prayer shifts from effort to agreement, warfare loses its emotional weight. You stand—not because the battle suddenly disappeared, but because the victory was already secured. This is not denying the fight. It is learning to pray from the place of someone who knows the war has already been won.

What I'm sharing here is not theory—it's the place prayer had to move for me when effort stopped working.

Understanding spiritual warfare is only the beginning. Truth becomes powerful when it is practiced. What you have just read is meant to move from insight into action, from awareness into prayer. The prayers in this next section are not about learning new words or trying harder; they are about standing in what Christ has already secured. You are not approaching God from a place of lack, but from a place of authority and trust. These prayers are offered as guides, not scripts—meant to be spoken honestly, adapted personally, and prayed with confidence. As you move forward, allow the Holy Spirit to lead you, reminding you that you do not fight for victory, but from it.

SECTION II — PRAYERS FOR PERSONAL WARFARE

Personal battles are confronted with personal authority.

Once truth is established, it must be enforced. This section equips you with personal warfare prayers to confront fear, oppression, emotional wounds, and spiritual pressure at the individual level. These prayers are designed to help you stand, resist, and walk free in what Christ has already secured.

Prayer For Protection & Covering

Father God, I come before You standing firmly on Your Word, not on fear, not on circumstances, and not on what I see. I declare that Your Word is true, settled, and alive concerning me.

Father, I stand on Your Word in Psalm 91, which declares that You cover me with Your feathers, and under Your wings I find refuge. Your truth is my shield and my buckler. Because of this, I declare that I will not fear the terror by night, nor the arrow that flies by day. Fear has no authority over my life, because You are my covering.

I declare according to Psalm 121 that You are my keeper. You are my shade upon my right hand. The sun will not strike me by day, nor the moon by night. You preserve me from all evil, and You preserve my soul. You guard my going out and my coming in, from this time forth and forevermore. I declare that my life is watched, guarded, and kept by You.

Father, I declare Psalm 46:1 over my life right now. You are my refuge and my strength, a very present help in trouble. I receive Your help in this moment, and I refuse to carry what You have already offered to bear.

Father, I take hold of Your promise and silence fear at its root. Your Word says, "Fear thou not; for I am with thee: be not dismayed; for I am thy God: I will strengthen thee; yea, I will help thee; yea, I will uphold thee with the right hand of my righteousness" (Isaiah 41:10). I reject intimidation, anxiety, and spiritual pressure. I receive Your strength. I receive Your help. I receive Your steady hand. I will not be shaken.

You have declared Yourself to be my hiding place. "Thou art my hiding place; thou shalt preserve me from trouble; thou shalt compass me about with songs of deliverance" (Psalm 32:7). I decree that no trouble sent against me will overtake me, and no plan formed against me will succeed. I am surrounded—not by fear, but by deliverance.

In the authority of Jesus Christ, I declare that every plan of the enemy formed against my life is restrained and rendered ineffective. Every attempt to bring fear, distraction, or harm is blocked by Your covering. I declare that no door is left open to the enemy, and no assignment has permission to remain. I stand covered by the blood of Jesus and guarded by Your truth.

I seal this prayer knowing that You are faithful to Your Word. I declare these things settled, established, and complete in the mighty name of Jesus Christ, Amen.

Prayer To Break Fear, Anxiety & Tormenting Spirits

Father God, I come to You standing on truth, and not the pressure of what I feel. I declare that fear has no legal authority in my life. You have not given me a spirit of fear, but of power, love, and a sound mind. Therefore, I reject fear at its root, and I refuse to partner with anxiety, torment, or intimidation in any form.

I declare according to Your Word that Jesus Christ has already disarmed principalities and powers, making a public spectacle of them and triumphing over them through the cross (Colossians 2:15). Because of this finished work, I do not fight for freedom—I enforce it. Every spirit of fear, heaviness, panic, oppression, and torment that attempts to operate in my mind, emotions, or body is confronted by the authority of Jesus Christ and commanded to leave. You have no permission here.

Your Word declares that You have not called me to live under torment. "There is no fear in love; but perfect love casteth out fear: because fear hath torment" (1 John 4:18). I receive Your perfect love right now, and I declare that torment is broken. Anxiety does not get to stay. Mental unrest does not get to rule. I choose peace—the peace that passes understanding—and I declare it guards my heart and my mind through Christ Jesus.

Father, I declare that I have the mind of Christ. I reject every lie, accusation, memory, or intrusive thought that does not agree with Your truth. I take captive every thought and bring it into obedience to Christ. My mind is not a battlefield for fear—it is a dwelling place for truth and peace. I declare that my thoughts align with heaven, not with worry.

Your Word says that I am more than a conqueror through Christ who loves me (Romans 8:37). I declare that I am not overwhelmed, not overtaken, and not defeated. Greater is He who lives in me than anything that comes against me (1 John 4:4).

In the authority of Jesus Christ, I break agreement with fear learned through trauma, sustained through stress, or reinforced through past experiences. What entered through pain will not remain through permission. I close every door fear has used to operate, and I declare my inner life restored to peace, stability, and confidence in You.

I declare that my home, my body, my sleep, my thoughts, and my emotions are covered by the peace of God. No tormenting presence is allowed to linger. No shadow of fear is allowed to remain. I am surrounded by the presence of the Holy Spirit, and where the Spirit of the Lord is, there is liberty.

I seal this prayer in faith, knowing that whom the Son sets free is free indeed. I move forward clear-minded and grounded in truth. In the mighty and authoritative name of Jesus Christ, Amen.

Prayer For Deliverance From Oppression & Heavy Burdens

Father God, I come before You standing on truth, not under weight. I refuse to carry what You never asked me to bear. Your Word declares that You are the lifter of my head, and today I receive that lifting. Every burden that has pressed on my spirit, every heaviness that has clouded my joy, every weight that has slowed my walk with You—I bring it before You now, not as a request for permission, but as an act of release.

Your Word says, "Come unto me, all ye that labour and are heavy laden, and I will give you rest" (Matthew 11:28). I respond to that invitation right now. I lay down emotional weight, spiritual pressure, mental exhaustion, and unspoken grief. I refuse to normalize heaviness that You call me to surrender. I exchange this weight for Your rest, this pressure for Your peace, and this burden for Your strength.

I declare that oppression has no authority over my life. Jesus Christ came to proclaim liberty to the captives and to set at liberty those who are bruised (Luke 4:18). Therefore, I enforce that liberty now. Every oppressive spirit, every heaviness assigned to discourage, delay, or drain me is confronted by the authority of Jesus Christ and commanded to lift and leave. You are not permitted to remain.

Your Word declares that You give "the garment of praise for the spirit of heaviness" (Isaiah 61:3). I receive that exchange right now. I clothe myself in praise. I praise You because You are faithful. I praise You because You are near. I praise You because You do not abandon Your people under pressure. Heaviness breaks where praise rises, and I declare that this atmosphere is shifting.

Father, I declare that the yoke is destroyed because of the anointing (Isaiah 10:27). Every yoke of emotional bondage, spiritual fatigue, and lingering sorrow is broken and destroyed. I will not live bent under weight when You have called me to walk upright in freedom.

I declare that I am not alone in this battle. You are my refuge and my strength. You are helping now. I refuse isolation, and I reject the lie that I must endure this quietly. You are with me, and Your presence lifts what human strength never could.

In the authority of Jesus Christ, I break agreement with despair, hopelessness, and silent suffering. I declare that joy is being restored, clarity is returning, and strength is rising. What has been heavy will not define me. What has pressed on me will not follow me forward.

I seal this prayer knowing that You are faithful to complete the work You have begun in me. I rise lighter, freer, and steadier than I came—because You are the burden-bearer, and I trust You fully. In the mighty name of Jesus Christ, Amen.

Prayer For Peace Of Mind & Sound Sleep

Father God, I come before You refusing unrest and receiving Your peace. I will not allow my mind to remain crowded with worry, replay, or unrest when You have already spoken rest over me. Your Word declares that You keep him in perfect peace whose mind is stayed on You, because he trusts in You (Isaiah 26:3). Tonight, I deliberately set my mind on You.

I declare that my mind belongs to Christ. You have not given me a spirit of fear, but of power, love, and a sound mind (2 Timothy 1:7). Therefore, I reject racing thoughts, intrusive memories, mental noise, and anxious anticipation of the future. Every thought that does not align with Your truth is brought into obedience to Christ. I do not negotiate with unrest. I replace it with truth.

Your Word promises that You give Your beloved sleep (Psalm 127:2). I receive that promise now. Sleep is not something I must force or earn—it is something You freely give. I declare that my body responds to peace and comes into alignment with rest. I release the tension I have been carrying and allow Your peace to settle over me completely.

I stand on Your Word that says, "When thou liest down, thou shalt not be afraid: yea, thou shalt lie down, and thy sleep shall be sweet" (Proverbs 3:24). I receive sweet sleep now. Restful sleep. Undisturbed sleep. Sleep that restores my strength and renews my mind. As I lie down, I am not exposed—I am covered. I am not vulnerable—I am guarded. I declare that no fear enters my thoughts, no disturbance invades my rest, and no spiritual interference disrupts what You have ordained.

Father, I thank You that even while I sleep, You are at work. You neither slumber nor sleep, and because You are my keeper, I can rest fully (Psalm 121:3–4). I stay sober and vigilant, but I refuse to live burdened by fear, because You are watching over me.

I stand alert, yet at rest, because You are my defense.

In the authority of Jesus Christ, I silence every assignment of restlessness, fear, and night torment. I declare that this atmosphere is filled with peace. My room is covered in the blood of Jesus. My mind is quiet. My body is at ease. I rest under the shadow of the Almighty and I dwell in the shelter of the Most High.

I seal this prayer with confidence, knowing that what I have declared according to Your Word is established. I lie down in peace, and I rise renewed. In the mighty name of Jesus Christ I pray, Amen.

Prayer For Emotional Healing & Inner Wounds

Father God, I come before You in the authority of Jesus Christ, not as a victim of my past, but as Your redeemed child. I stand on truth, not on trauma. I stand on Your Word, not on wounds. You are Jehovah Rapha—the Lord who heals—and I call on You now to intervene in every place where my soul has been injured, burdened, or bound.

Father, I bring before You every wound caused by rejection—rejection from people, rejection from authority, rejection from family, rejection from relationships, rejection that shaped how I see myself and how I expect others to treat me. I renounce the lie that rejection speaks over my identity. I declare that I am chosen, accepted, and loved in Christ Jesus.

In the name of Jesus Christ, I bind and command every spirit of rejection, fear, confusion, heaviness, despair, and depression that entered through trauma, abandonment, betrayal, or loss—you no longer have permission to remain. I break your assignment now. You will not operate in my mind, my emotions, my body, or my future. I command you to leave completely and permanently by the authority of Jesus Christ.

Father, I ask for divine intervention at the deepest levels of my soul. Heal emotional trauma that words never touched. Heal wounds that time did not fix. Heal places I learned to survive instead of live. Where trauma disrupted my peace, restore peace. Where fear settled into my nervous system, bring calm. Where emotional exhaustion weakened my heart, renew my strength.

I speak healing over my body now. I declare balance over hormones, peace over my nerves, rest over my mind, and strength over my heart. I declare that my body responds to truth, not trauma. I declare that stress, anxiety, and emotional overload will no longer rule my physical health.

Father, by the blood of Jesus, cleanse every place where pain attached itself. Let the blood of Jesus wash, heal, restore, and seal every wounded area of my soul. I declare that the blood of Jesus surrounds me, fills me, covers me, and delivers me from every lingering effect of trauma, rejection, and bondage.

I declare supernatural renewal now. Restore what was lost—time, peace, confidence, health, joy, relationships, and dreams. Your Word says You restore the years the locust has eaten, and I receive that restoration. I declare divine reversals over my life. What the enemy used to harm me, You are turning for my good.

Father, shatter every demonic chain that formed through pain, fear, or rejection. Break every internal agreement I made with lies in moments of hurt. I cancel them now in the name of Jesus. I align my heart, my mind, and my identity with truth.

Holy Spirit, fill every place that healing touches. Where wounds once lived, bring Your presence. Where emptiness remained, bring Your comfort. Guide me as I walk forward healed, whole, and strengthened. Lead me into peace. Lead me into truth. Lead me into rest.

I declare that I am no longer defined by what hurt me. I am healed by the hands of God. I am restored by His power. I am free by the blood of Jesus.

> I break and renounce every agreement made with rejection, abandonment, and unworthiness, in the name of Jesus Christ.

> I cancel every belief formed in pain that told me I was unwanted, unsafe, unseen, or unloved.

> I break agreement with shame and self-protection that formed as a response to pain.

> I renounce every vow made in fear—every promise to shut down, withdraw, overachieve, or self-protect apart from God.

I break agreement with fear, anxiety, despair, and hopelessness, and I declare they no longer have legal access to my life.

I cancel every agreement with trauma that tried to shape my identity, my expectations, or my future.

I renounce every word spoken over me or by me that contradicted God's truth about who I am.

I declare that my soul now agrees with the truth of God's Word, the work of the cross, and the finished victory of Jesus Christ.

By the power of the blood of Jesus, I revoke every legal right given to the enemy through these agreements. I command every spirit that operated through them to leave now. You no longer have access. You no longer have influence. Your assignment is broken in the name of Jesus Christ.

I seal this prayer by faith, knowing that what You begin, You complete.

In the mighty, healing, delivering name of Jesus Christ, Amen.

Prayer For Discernment & Spiritual Clarity

Father God, I come before You in the authority of Jesus Christ, asking not for information, but for revelation. I ask You to sharpen my spiritual sight and quiet every competing voice that has blurred my ability to hear You clearly. You are not a God of confusion, but of peace, and I declare that clarity belongs to me as Your child.

Father, I ask that You cleanse my spiritual perception. Remove every filter formed by fear, trauma, disappointment, or misunderstanding. Heal places where past pain distorted my discernment and caused me to misread people, situations, or Your voice. Where confusion settled in, bring order. Where uncertainty lingered, release confidence. Where I have doubted Your leading, realign my heart with truth.

In the name of Jesus Christ, I bind and silence every spirit of confusion, deception, distraction, delay, and spiritual fog. I cancel every assignment sent to distort truth, twist perception, limit vision, or keep me circling when You have already prepared a path forward. You have no authority over my mind, my decisions, or my discernment. I command every counterfeit voice to be exposed, confronted, and removed.

Father, I ask for Your wisdom—the kind that comes from above, pure, peaceable, and full of truth. Anoint my mind with clarity and my spirit with understanding. Let the fire of the Holy Spirit burn away every limitation the enemy tried to place on my vision. Break fear-based hesitation. Break delay rooted in doubt. Break every spiritual ceiling that has kept me from fully walking in Your will.

Teach me to discern truth from deception, Your purposes from my preferences, and Your timing from my impatience. Where I have mistaken desire for direction, correct me. Where I have leaned on my own understanding, bring me back into dependence on You. I choose Your will over my comfort, Your voice over my assumptions, and Your way over my own.

I declare that I have the mind of Christ. I take captive every thought that rises against the knowledge of God, and I bring it into obedience to Christ. I declare that my thoughts are aligned with truth, my emotions are submitted to wisdom, and my decisions are led by the Holy Spirit. I will not be ruled by impulse, pressure, or fear.

I declare that Your Word is a lamp unto my feet and a light unto my path. As I stay grounded in Scripture, train my spiritual senses to recognize what is from You and what is not. Give me discernment that is steady, not suspicious; wisdom that is peaceful, not anxious; clarity that draws me closer to You, not farther away.

Father, expose anything in my life that looks harmless but carries compromise. Reveal subtle deception, misplaced trust, unhealthy attachments, and spiritual mixtures that weaken discernment. Where something has sounded right but produced unrest, give me the courage to step back. Where I have tolerated what You never approved, lead me into repentance and realignment.

Holy Spirit, speak clearly and consistently. Tune my ears to recognize Your voice above every other influence. Let Your guidance be unmistakable. Order my steps. Confirm Your direction. When You say move, I will move. When You say wait, I will wait. When You say let go, I will release without fear.

I declare that I walk in light, and darkness has no hiding place in my life. I declare that confusion has no authority here. I declare that truth is established, wisdom is active, and clarity governs my decisions. I walk in the anointing to see clearly, choose wisely, and follow faithfully.

I seal this prayer by faith, trusting that You are faithful to guide me into all truth. I receive discernment. I receive wisdom. I receive clarity.

In the mighty, wise, and victorious name of Jesus Christ, Amen.

SECTION III — PRAYERS FOR BREAKTHROUGH

What has resisted you will not outlast God's power.

Some battles require targeted prayer to break long-standing patterns and stubborn resistance. This section focuses on tearing down barriers, shattering cycles, and releasing God-ordained movement where stagnation once existed. Here, you move from survival into forward momentum.

Prayer To Break Generational Curses

Father God, I come before You in the authority of Jesus Christ, not as a product of my bloodline, but as a new creation in Christ. I stand on the finished work of the cross, and I declare that my lineage has been interrupted by redemption. Your Word declares, "Christ hath redeemed us from the curse of the law, being made a curse for us" (Galatians 3:13). Because of Jesus, I am no longer under any generational curse—I am under covenant blessing.

Father, I acknowledge that patterns did not begin with me, but I declare they end with me. In the name of Jesus Christ, I renounce and break every generational curse operating through my bloodline—known and unknown, spoken and unspoken, intentional or inherited. I separate myself now from every ancestral chain tied to sin, rebellion, trauma, and disobedience.

By the authority of Jesus Christ and the power of His blood, I renounce every bloodline covenant that did not originate from You. I break agreement with ancestral covenants tied to idolatry, occult practices, witchcraft, divination, secret societies, freemasonry, fraternities, sororities, ungodly vows, and spoken curses. I break agreement from every verbal, written, blood oath, pledge, contract, agreement, and covenant. I declare that no covenant made in darkness has authority over me. The blood of Jesus speaks a better word over my life.

In the name of Jesus Christ, I specifically break generational curses of poverty, lack, and financial limitation. I renounce every inherited mindset of scarcity, failure, and loss. I break cycles of debt, struggle, and financial instability. I declare that I am not destined to repeat hardship. I receive God's provision, favor, and abundance according to His will.

I break generational curses of sickness, disease, and infirmity. I renounce patterns of chronic illness, unexplained conditions, mental illness, depression, anxiety, addiction, and emotional instability that have followed my bloodline. I declare that sickness does not have permission to pass through me to the next generation. By the stripes of Jesus Christ, I receive healing and wholeness.

I break generational curses of rejection, abandonment, broken relationships, and identity confusion. I renounce the lie that I am unwanted, overlooked, or unworthy. I declare that rejection will not define my life, my relationships, or my future. I am chosen, accepted, and beloved in Christ Jesus.

In the name of Jesus, I bind and command every familiar spirit, ancestral spirit, and demonic attachment operating through my bloodline to be broken and removed. You no longer have legal access, influence, or permission to operate in my life. Every stronghold built through generations—I command you to fall now. Every chain—I command you to break. Every residue—I command you to be consumed by the fire of God.

Father, I apply the blood of Jesus over my bloodline—past, present, and future. Let the blood cleanse, cover, and separate me from every curse, every pattern, and every consequence of generational sin. I declare that my bloodline is redeemed, realigned, and restored through Christ.

I declare a divine reversal. Where there was loss, release restoration. Where there was shame, release honor. Where there was limitation, release favor. Where there was failure, release fruitfulness. Your Word declares that You bless to a thousand generations those who love You, and I receive that promise now.

I declare that I walk in freedom. I declare that I walk in blessing. I declare that I walk in a new inheritance. I am no longer bound by what came before me. I am led by the Spirit of God, covered by the blood of Jesus, and established in righteousness.

I seal this prayer by faith, knowing that what You break cannot be rebuilt, and what You redeem cannot be reclaimed by the enemy.

In the mighty, victorious, delivering name of Jesus Christ, Amen.

Prayer Against Witchcraft, Word Curses & Evil Altars

Father God, I come before You in the authority of Jesus Christ, standing on the finished work of the cross. I do not approach You in fear, but in confidence, knowing that the victory has already been secured. Your Word declares that You are a consuming fire, and I call upon that holy fire now. "For our God is a consuming fire" (Hebrews 12:29).

In the name of Jesus Christ, I come against every form of witchcraft, sorcery, divination, familiar spirits, and occult influence working against my life, my family, or my destiny. I declare that no power of darkness has authority over me. I belong to Jesus Christ, and I am covered by His blood.

Father, Your Word says that Jesus "blotted out the handwriting of ordinances that was against us... and having spoiled principalities and powers, He made a shew of them openly, triumphing over them" (Colossians 2:14–15). By that same authority, I declare that every evil record, accusation, judgment, or declaration made against me at any altar, shrine, or place of darkness is erased by the blood of Jesus.

In the name of Jesus Christ, I command the blood of Jesus to cancel, nullify, and silence every word curse, spell, incantation, chant, or declaration spoken against my life—whether spoken knowingly or unknowingly, recently or in the past. I declare that no weapon formed against me shall prosper, and every tongue that rises against me in judgment is condemned, as written in Isaiah 54:17.

By the fire of the Holy Ghost, I command every evil altar raised against my destiny to be consumed now. Let the fire of God fall and shatter altars built by household enemies, bloodline ancestors, or occult practitioners. Let every sacrifice offered against my life be overturned. Let every demonic agreement tied to my foundation be dissolved by fire.

In the name of Jesus, I blind every familiar spirit assigned to monitor my progress, my family, my calling, or my future. You will not track me. You will not report on me. You will not interfere with what God has ordained. I declare that my life is hidden with Christ in God.

Father, let the thunder of God break every ancestral covenant and demonic agreement tied to witchcraft, idolatry, or bloodline rituals. Let every judgment passed against my destiny at an evil altar be reversed by the righteous judgment of Heaven. I declare divine reversals now—what was spoken for harm is turned for good.

Your Word declares, "They overcame him by the blood of the Lamb, and by the word of their testimony" (Revelation 12:11). By the blood of Jesus, I overcome every work of witchcraft, every occult manipulation, and every hidden agenda of darkness. I declare that I am redeemed, released, and restored.

Father, I declare that no curse can stand where the blood speaks. I declare that no fire of darkness can survive where Your fire burns. I declare that my destiny is protected, my path is cleared, and my future is secured in Christ.

I declare that every curse spoken against me is canceled by the blood of Jesus.

I declare that no spell, incantation, or evil word has power over my life.

I declare that every evil altar raised against my destiny is destroyed by the fire of God.

I declare that every demonic agreement and ancestral covenant is broken and dissolved.

I declare that familiar spirits assigned to monitor me are blinded and silenced.

I declare that my life is hidden with Christ in God and cannot be accessed by darkness.

I declare that every judgment spoken against my future is reversed by Heaven.

I declare that witchcraft works against me fail and collapse completely.

I declare that the blood of Jesus speaks louder than any voice raised against me.

I declare that my destiny is protected, my path is cleared, and my future is secure.

I declare that I walk in freedom, authority, and victory through Jesus Christ.

I declare that this work is finished, sealed, and enforced by Heaven.

I seal this prayer by the blood of Jesus and declare it finished, irreversible, and enforced by Heaven. In the mighty, victorious name of Jesus Christ, Amen.

Prayer For Financial Breakthrough & Overflow

Father God, I come before You in the authority of Jesus Christ, standing on Your Word and not on lack, fear, or past failure. You are Jehovah Jireh—my Provider—and I declare that You are faithful to supply every need according to Your riches in glory by Christ Jesus. I refuse to see my life through scarcity. I align my faith with Heaven's provision.

Father, Your Word declares, "The LORD is my shepherd; I shall not want" (Psalm 23:1). Because You lead my life, lack does not have the final word. I reject the lie that I will always struggle, always fall short, or always live beneath what You promised. I declare that want, insufficiency, and financial pressure lose their grip on my life now.

In the name of Jesus Christ, I break every spirit of poverty, lack, debt, and financial oppression that has tried to attach itself to my life, my family, or my bloodline. I renounce every agreement made with fear, survival mentality, and limitation. I cancel every pattern of financial loss and inherited struggle, and I declare a generational shift now. Your Word says, "A good man leaveth an inheritance to his children's children: and the wealth of the sinner is laid up for the just" (Proverbs 13:22). I receive that inheritance mindset. I declare that what was meant to drain my family line is now redirected for godly legacy, stability, and blessing.

Father, I declare Your Word in Malachi 3:10, that as I walk in obedience, You open the windows of heaven and pour out blessing that there will not be room enough to receive it. I declare that every devourer assigned to my finances is rebuked now. What was leaking is sealed. What was delayed is released. What was blocked is opened.

Your Word also declares, "Moreover the profit of the earth is for all: the king himself is served by the field" (Ecclesiastes 5:9). I receive this truth—that You have established provision within the earth itself. I declare that the systems, resources, and opportunities You have ordained for my provision begin to align with me now. I reject the lie that there is no way forward. You have already placed supply in the field, and You are directing my steps toward it.

Father, You said, "But thou shalt remember the LORD thy God: for it is he that giveth thee power to get wealth" (Deuteronomy 8:18). I receive that power now. I receive divine ideas, insight, strategy, discipline, and favor. I declare that my hands are blessed, my work is productive, and my efforts yield increase. I will not labor in vain.

I speak to every financial delay, closed door, and withheld resource, and I command you to align with the will of God. I declare acceleration where there has been delay, restoration where there has been loss, and overflow where there has only been enough. I declare that what the enemy intended to drain, God is using to multiply.

Father, Your Word declares that You are able "to do exceeding abundantly above all that we ask or think, according to the power that worketh in us" (Ephesians 3:20). I receive overflow not just for my needs, but so I can be a blessing. I will lend and not borrow. I will give freely and joyfully. I will walk in generosity without fear.

I declare that my finances come into divine order. I declare peace replaces pressure. Provision replaces panic. Wisdom replaces confusion. Faith replaces fear. I declare that my life reflects the goodness of God and the faithfulness of His promises.

I seal this prayer by faith, knowing that Heaven has heard and responded. I declare breakthrough is released, provision is flowing, and overflow is established.

In the mighty, providing, victorious name of Jesus Christ, Amen.

Prayer For Healing & Physical Restoration

Father God, I come before You in the authority of Jesus Christ, not as one begging for relief, but as one standing on covenant truth. You are Jehovah Rapha—the Lord who heals (Exodus 15:26), and You have revealed Yourself as the God who "healeth all thy diseases" (Psalm 103:3). I take my stand on Your Word, and I declare that my body belongs to You.

In the name of Jesus Christ, I address every root of sickness, affliction, pain, and physical disorder operating in my body. I declare that no illness is permitted to remain hidden or unchallenged. Your Word declares that "every plant, which my heavenly Father hath not planted, shall be rooted up" (Matthew 15:13). I expose every spiritual root—whether generational, ancestral, environmental, emotional, or demonic—that is feeding disease or weakness in my body, and I command it to be uprooted now.

By the fire of the Holy Ghost, I call for every ungodly root tied to generational curses, ancestral idol worship, inherited sickness, bloodline affliction, or demonic oppression to be consumed and burnt away. Your Word declares that "our God is a consuming fire" (Hebrews 12:29). I sever every tie connecting my body to sickness passed down through family lines. I declare that generational infirmity ends with me. I am not a carrier of disease—I am a carrier of God's glory.

In the name of Jesus, I break and renounce every ungodly soul tie, demonic attachment, or spiritual access point that has been using my body as a place of affliction. I command every spirit of infirmity, pain, weakness, and decay to loose its hold and leave my body now. Jesus declared that He came "to destroy the works of the devil" (1 John 3:8), and I enforce that victory right now. You have no legal right. You have no authority. You have no permission to remain.

I plead the blood of Jesus over my body right now—from the crown of my head to the soles of my feet. Your Word declares that "the blood of Jesus Christ His Son cleanseth us from all sin" (1 John 1:7), and I declare that same blood cleanses every cell, every tissue, every organ, and every system in my body. I declare that the blood of Jesus speaks *"better things"* over me (Hebrews 12:24)—healing, restoration, and life. Where there has been damage, the blood rebuilds. Where there has been inflammation, the blood calms. Where there has been deterioration, the blood restores.

By the authority of Jesus Christ, I speak to my body and command alignment with Heaven. Your Word says that "life and death are in the power of the tongue" (Proverbs 18:21), and I release life now. I declare that abnormal cells are corrected by the power of God. I declare that blocked arteries open, circulation is restored, and organs function as God designed them. I declare that nerves are healed, bones are strengthened, muscles are restored, and every system comes into divine order.

Father, let Your manifest presence fill me now. Your Word declares that "in Thy presence is fullness of joy" (Psalm 16:11), and I declare that where Your presence enters, sickness must exit. When Your glory fills this temple, every foreign substance—whether spiritual or physical—must leave. "The light shineth in darkness; and the darkness comprehended it not" (John 1:5). Disease cannot survive where Your Spirit reigns.

Your Word declares that "Surely He hath borne our griefs, and carried our sorrows" (Isaiah 53:4), and that "by His stripes we are healed" (Isaiah 53:5; 1 Peter 2:24). I receive that healing now—not as a future hope, but as a present reality. I declare that my body responds to the Word of God. I declare restoration, renewal, and strength released now.

Holy Spirit, saturate every place healing touches. Seal this work. Sustain it. Complete it. Your Word promises that "He which hath begun a good work in you will perform it until the day of Jesus Christ" (Philippians 1:6). Teach my body how to remain aligned with truth and life. I declare that my body is the temple of the Holy Ghost (1 Corinthians 6:19), and it will function in health, strength, and wholeness.

I seal this prayer by faith, knowing that what God begins, He finishes. Healing is released. Restoration is established. Life flows freely in my body.

In the mighty, healing, resurrecting name of Jesus Christ, Amen.

Prayer For Open Doors & God-Ordained Opportunities

Father God, I come before You in the authority of Jesus Christ, standing on covenant and not on limitation. You are the God who orders my steps (Psalm 37:23), and I acknowledge You as the One who opens doors that no man can shut and shuts doors no man can open. Your Word declares, "Behold, I have set before thee an open door, and no man can shut it" (Revelation 3:8), and I receive that Word as active and alive over my life right now.

Father, I ask for divine intervention in every area where progress has been delayed, restricted, or resisted. I call for breakthroughs that only You can orchestrate. Where there have been barriers, blockages, closed systems, or invisible resistance, I ask You to move by Your power. Your Word says, "For God is the one who opens doors no one can close, and closes doors no one can open" (Job 12:14). I declare that no opposition has the authority to override Your will for my life.

In the name of Jesus Christ, I reject every limitation rooted in fear, past failure, rejection, delay, or discouragement. I break agreement with small thinking, restricted vision, and inherited ceilings. Your Word declares that "The path of the just is as the shining light, that shineth more and more unto the perfect day" (Proverbs 4:18). I declare forward movement. I declare expansion. I declare clarity and momentum where there was once confusion and stagnation.

Father, I ask You to release divine favor over my life. Your Word says, "For thou, LORD, wilt bless the righteous; with favour wilt thou compass him as with a shield" (Psalm 5:12). I declare that favor speaks for me where my voice cannot reach. Favor opens doors that credentials cannot open. Favor positions me where preparation meets opportunity. I declare that I am recognized, remembered, and recommended by the right people at the right time.

Lord, connect me with destiny helpers—people You have already assigned to my journey. Remove every counterfeit connection and misaligned relationship that delays purpose. Your Word says, "A man's gift maketh room for him, and bringeth him before great men" (Proverbs 18:16). I declare that what You have placed inside of me makes room for me. I will not miss my moment. I will not overlook divine connections. I will not be hidden when it is time to be seen.

Holy Spirit, empower me to walk boldly through every door You open. Your Word declares, "Not by might, nor by power, but by my Spirit, saith the LORD of hosts" (Zechariah 4:6). I ask for courage to step into new seasons without fear. Give me wisdom to discern timing, clarity to recognize opportunity, and obedience to move when You say move. I refuse hesitation rooted in doubt. I choose faith, alignment, and trust.

Father, I declare that this is a new season. Your Word declares, "Forget the former things; behold, I will do a new thing; now it shall spring forth" (Isaiah 43:18–19). I release the past. I step out of old cycles. I embrace what You are doing now. I declare that doors connected to my calling, purpose, provision, and assignment are opening in sequence and order.

I declare that no demonic resistance, delay, or opposition can stop what You have ordained. "If God be for us, who can be against us?" (Romans 8:31). I move forward with confidence, knowing that You go before me, You stand beside me, and You secure what concerns me. "The LORD will perfect that which concerneth me" (Psalm 138:8).

I seal this prayer by faith, declaring that open doors are manifesting, divine opportunities are aligning, and God-ordained favor is resting on my life. I walk forward ready, willing, and obedient. In the mighty name of Jesus Christ, Amen.

Prayer To Break Cycles Of Delay & Denial

Father God, I come before You by faith in Jesus Christ, refusing to accept stagnation, limitation, or prolonged resistance as my portion. I reject delay, denial, and repeated obstruction, and I appeal to heaven for divine intervention in every area of my life where progress has been challenged. You are the God who speaks—and when You speak, nothing can delay the fulfillment of Your word.

In the name of Jesus Christ, I confront every cycle of delay operating in my life—whether rooted in generational patterns, spiritual opposition, rejection, disobedience, or past failure. Your Word declares, "There shall none of my words be prolonged any more, but the word which I have spoken shall be done, saith the Lord GOD" (Ezekiel 12:28). I declare that delay is not my inheritance. I break every inherited pattern of stagnation, missed opportunities, and prolonged struggle. What followed my bloodline stops with me.

Father, I speak directly to every force assigned to hinder my movement forward. Every spirit of delay, denial, setback, confusion, and frustration—you are exposed and stripped of authority now. Your Word says, "Thou shalt decree a thing, and it shall be established unto thee" (Job 22:28). I decree acceleration where there was delay. I decree approval where there was denial. I decree progress where there was resistance.

Lord, I ask for divine restoration of time, opportunity, and momentum. Your Word declares, "I will restore to you the years that the locust hath eaten" (Joel 2:25). I receive restoration of lost seasons, delayed breakthroughs, deferred dreams, and postponed victories. What was held back is released. What was slowed is now moving. What was denied is now granted according to Your will.

Father, where rejection has blocked advancement, I declare acceptance. Where "no" has echoed repeatedly, I declare a divinely ordered "yes." Your Word says, "The stone which the builders refused is become the head stone of the corner" (Psalm 118:22). I declare that rejection is being transformed into elevation. What disqualified me in the eyes of man is qualifying me by the hand of God.

I step out of old cycles and into new beginnings. Your Word declares, "If any man be in Christ, he is a new creature: old things are passed away; behold, all things are become new" (2 Corinthians 5:17). I declare that this is a new season—new clarity, new favor, new momentum, and new alignment. I am no longer circling the same mountain. I am moving forward into purpose.

Father, I release light into every place where delay once lingered. Your Word declares, "And the light shineth in darkness; and the darkness comprehended it not" (John 1:5). I declare that confusion, resistance, and stagnation are giving way to clarity and forward movement. Darkness cannot stop what You have ordained. Delay cannot outlast divine light.

By the power of the Holy Spirit, I declare divine forward movement now. Doors are opening. Help is arriving. Favor is speaking. Resistance is breaking. I will not miss my moment. I will not arrive late to what God has prepared. I align my steps with heaven's timing and receive grace for obedience and courage.

I seal this prayer by faith, declaring that cycles are broken, delays are lifted, denials are overturned, and victory is established. I walk forward free, aligned, and confident in the finished work of Jesus Christ. In the mighty name of Jesus Christ, Amen.

SECTION IV — PRAYERS FOR THE HOME & FAMILY

What God establishes in you, He also establishes in your house.

Warfare does not stop with the individual—it extends to what you steward.

This section covers your household, relationships, children, and family bloodline with prayer, protection, and divine order. What God establishes in you, He also desires to establish in your house.

Prayer For Household Protection

Father God, I come before You in the authority of Jesus Christ, standing as a gatekeeper over my home and family. I declare that this house belongs to You. It is set apart, marked, and claimed for the glory of God. Every right of access given to darkness—knowingly or unknowingly—is revoked now by the blood of Jesus.

Father, I invoke Your fiery presence to surround this home. Let the fire of the Holy Ghost rise as a wall of protection around every door, every window, every room, and every boundary of this property. Your Word declares, "For I, saith the LORD, will be unto her a wall of fire round about, and will be the glory in the midst of her" (Zechariah 2:5). I declare that no evil can cross what You have set ablaze with Your presence.

I plead the blood of Jesus over this household—over every family member, every child, every relationship, every possession, and every future assignment connected to this home. By the blood of Jesus, I break every curse, cancel every demonic agreement, and nullify every sacrifice, spell, chant, or word spoken against this family. The blood of Jesus speaks better things, and it speaks peace, protection, and deliverance over us now.

Father, I dismantle by the authority of Jesus Christ every demonic altar raised against this home—whether built through ancestral sin, witchcraft, jealousy, envy, or spiritual opposition. Let the fire of God consume every altar of darkness, every foundation of affliction, and every claim of the enemy. Your Word declares, "No weapon that is formed against thee shall prosper" (Isaiah 54:17), and I enforce that promise over this house.

Lord, I ask You to release angelic protection over my home. Your Word says, "For he shall give his angels charge over thee, to keep thee in all thy ways" (Psalm 91:11). I ask for warrior angels to stand guard, messenger angels to bring divine instruction, and ministering angels to bring provision, peace, and order into this household. Let angels encamp around us, just as it is written: "The angel of the LORD encampeth round about them that fear him, and delivereth them" (Psalm 34:7).

In the name of Jesus Christ, I rebuke every demonic plan, every monitoring spirit, every familiar spirit, every form of witchcraft, and every assignment sent to observe, harass, or infiltrate this household. You are exposed, restrained, and commanded to leave now. You have no authority here. This home is sealed by the blood of Jesus and guarded by the power of God.

Father, I declare Psalm 91 over this home. We dwell in the secret place of the Most High, and we abide under the shadow of the Almighty. You are our refuge and our fortress. No terror by night, no arrow by day, no pestilence, no destruction, and no unseen attack shall come near this dwelling. This home is preserved by You.

I declare protection over our children—their minds, their bodies, their emotions, and their futures. I declare peace over our relationships, wisdom over our decisions, and unity within our walls. Where the enemy attempted division, You establish harmony. Where chaos tried to enter, You release peace.

Father, open doors of divine favor, promotion, provision, and breakthrough for this household—doors that no man can shut. And I ask You to close every door that would bring harm, distraction, delay, or compromise. Lead this family by Your Spirit and establish us in righteousness.

I declare that this home is a dwelling place for the presence of God. It is a house of peace, prayer, protection, and blessing. Darkness has no residence here. Confusion has no voice here. Fear has no authority here.

I seal this prayer by faith, knowing that You are faithful to Your Word and mighty to defend what belongs to You. In the mighty, victorious name of Jesus Christ, Amen.

Prayer for Children & the Next Generation

Father God, I come before You in the authority of Jesus Christ, standing on behalf of my children and the generations that will come from my bloodline. Your Word says, "Lo, children are an heritage of the LORD: and the fruit of the womb is his reward" (Psalm 127:3). I declare today that my children belong to You. Their lives, their futures, their destinies are not owned by fear, culture, trauma, or the enemy—they are claimed by God.

In the name of Jesus Christ, I plead the blood of Jesus over my children—over their minds, emotions, bodies, spirits, and futures. Your Word declares, "They overcame him by the blood of the Lamb, and by the word of their testimony" (Revelation 12:11). I declare that the blood of Jesus speaks louder than every word ever spoken against them. Every curse, label, judgment, or evil declaration released over my children or my family line is erased, canceled, and silenced by the blood of Jesus.

Father, I ask that You be a wall of fire around my children. As You have promised, "For I, saith the LORD, will be unto her a wall of fire round about, and will be the glory in the midst of her" (Zechariah 2:5). Surround them with Your presence day and night. Protect them from dangers they cannot yet see, battles they are not mature enough to recognize, and assignments of darkness formed against their lives. Your Word says, "No weapon that is formed against thee shall prosper; and every tongue that shall rise against thee in judgment thou shalt condemn" (Isaiah 54:17). I declare divine protection over my children now.

In the name of Jesus, I break every generational curse operating in my bloodline. Your Word declares, "The son shall not bear the iniquity of the father" (Ezekiel 18:20). I decree that ancestral sin, inherited trauma, and bloodline patterns have no legal authority over my children. Cycles of fear, failure, rejection, depression, confusion, addiction, poverty, and limitation are terminated now. What affected previous generations will not continue through my lineage. My children inherit freedom, not bondage; blessing, not burden; destiny, not delay.

I command every demonic assignment sent against my children's purpose to be destroyed now. Every spirit of fear, intimidation, confusion, heaviness, delay, insecurity, and self-doubt—leave them now in the name of Jesus Christ. Your Word declares, "For God hath not given us the spirit of fear; but of power, and of love, and of a sound mind" (2 Timothy 1:7). I declare that my children walk in clarity, peace, confidence, and strength.

Father, I declare that You are ordering the steps of my children according to Your will. Your Word says, "A man's heart deviseth his way: but the LORD directeth his steps" (Proverbs 16:9). Go before them and remove obstacles they are not strong enough to move on their own. Open the right paths, close every dangerous door, and align them with divine opportunities, destiny helpers, and God-ordained connections. Lead them into the paths You prepared for them before they were born. As it is written, "Before I formed thee in the belly I knew thee; and before thou camest forth out of the womb I sanctified thee" (Jeremiah 1:5). Unlock their gifts. Strengthen their voices. Remove every limitation placed on their calling.

Holy Spirit, train my children to hear Your voice clearly. Your Word says, "My sheep hear my voice, and I know them, and they follow me" (John 10:27). Guide them when I cannot. Correct them when I am not present. Protect them from deception and lead them into truth. Let obedience become natural to them and Your presence familiar from an early age.

Father, fill my children with wisdom, courage, and discernment. Your Word promises, "If any of you lack wisdom, let him ask of God, that giveth to all men liberally" (James 1:5). Let their lives shine as light in dark places. "The path of the just is as the shining light, that shineth more and more unto the perfect day" (Proverbs 4:18). Use them for Your glory.

I declare that my children are taught by the Lord, and peace rests upon their lives. "All thy children shall be taught of the LORD; and great shall be the peace of thy children" (Isaiah 54:13). Their future is protected. Their destiny is secure. My bloodline will testify to the faithfulness of God.

I seal this prayer by faith, trusting that You watch over Your Word to perform it. In the mighty, protecting, destiny-shaping name of Jesus Christ, Amen.

Prayer for Marriages & Relationships

Father God, I come before You in the authority of Jesus Christ, submitting my relationships and my desires to Your perfect will. I declare that my life is led by the Spirit of God and not by emotion, impulse, fear, or the flesh. Your Word says, "As many as are led by the Spirit of God, they are the sons of God" (Romans 8:14), and I decree that every relationship connected to my life must come into alignment with Your Spirit and Your truth.

Father, I lift up my marriage—or the marriage You are preparing for me—and I declare that You are the foundation, the center, and the covering. Your Word declares, "Unless the LORD builds the house, they labor in vain who build it" (Psalm 127:1). I reject every counterfeit connection, every soul tie formed outside of Your will, and every relationship rooted in lust, insecurity, trauma, or fear of being alone. I ask You to purify my heart and my desires so that I choose alignment over attraction, obedience over emotion, and purpose over pressure.

In the name of Jesus, I come against every tactic of the enemy sent to bring division, confusion, strife, offense, betrayal, or emotional distance in marriages and relationships. Your Word declares, "What God has joined together, let no one separate" (Mark 10:9). I rebuke every spirit of division and fear. I silence the voice of accusation, misunderstanding, and pride. I declare peace, humility, forgiveness, and unity to reign where You have ordained covenant.

Father, I ask for healing where relationships have been wounded. Heal broken trust. Heal emotional fractures. Heal marriages strained by past hurts, unmet expectations, or spiritual disconnection. Your Word says You are "near to the brokenhearted and save those who are crushed in spirit" (Psalm 34:18). I invite Your restoring presence into every damaged place. Where love grew cold, reignite it by Your Spirit. Where communication broke down, restore understanding and grace.

Lord, for those believing You for a spouse, I ask that You manifest a kingdom spouse—one who fears You, walks in wisdom, and honors Your Word. Your Word declares, "He who finds a wife finds a good thing and obtains favor from the LORD" (Proverbs 18:22). I declare that my spouse is not a distraction but a divine partner in purpose. Align us spiritually before You connect us physically or emotionally. Let our union advance Your kingdom, sharpen our faith, and glorify Your name.

Holy Spirit, lead me daily. Guard my heart from lust, compromise, and fleshly desire. Your Word says, "Walk in the Spirit, and you shall not fulfill the lust of the flesh" (Galatians 5:16). Teach me to discern character over charm, fruit over feelings, and covenant over convenience. Let my relationships reflect holiness, peace, and righteousness.

Father, surround my marriage and relationships with Your presence, favor, and power. Place a hedge of protection around us. Let Your angels encamp around our union. I declare that no weapon formed against our love, our communication, or our covenant shall prosper. I choose relationships that bring me closer to You, not further from purpose.

I declare that my relationships are God-centered, Spirit-led, and destiny-aligned. I will love from a place of wholeness, not need. I will build with wisdom, not fear. I trust You completely with my heart, my future, and my relationships.

I seal this prayer in faith, believing that You are working all things together for my good and Your glory. In the mighty name of Jesus Christ, Amen.

Prayer For Peace In The Home

Father God, I come before You in the authority of Jesus Christ, inviting Your holy presence to dwell fully in my home. I declare that my house belongs to You. Your Word says, "As for me and my house, we will serve the LORD" (Joshua 24:15), and I decree that my home is not a place of strife, fear, or unrest, but a dwelling place for Your glory, Your peace, and Your Spirit.

Father, I ask that You release Your manifest presence into every room, every space, and every atmosphere within my home. Let Your peace rule here. Your Word declares, "The peace of God, which surpasses all understanding, will guard your hearts and your minds in Christ Jesus" (Philippians 4:7). I declare that anxiety, tension, confusion, and emotional heaviness have no authority here. Where chaos tried to settle, I speak divine order. Where unrest lingered, I release heaven's peace.

In the name of Jesus Christ, I break every negative spiritual chain attached to this home—every cycle of anger, division, fear, depression, exhaustion, or heaviness. I renounce every word spoken in frustration, every curse spoken in anger, and every negative declaration made knowingly or unknowingly. I declare that by the blood of Jesus, every evil word is canceled, every spiritual residue is cleansed, and every open door is shut.

Father, let the fire of the Holy Ghost surround and fill this home with Your holy presence. Your Word declares, "For our God is a consuming fire" (Hebrews 12:29). I declare that Your fire consumes every trace of darkness, drives out every demonic presence, silences every voice of fear, and destroys every assignment of the enemy. A home filled with Your fire and Your Word is untouchable by darkness.

I plead the blood of Jesus over this house now—over the doors, the windows, the walls, and every person who dwells here. Let the blood of Jesus cleanse, heal, cover, and deliver this home from every curse, every affliction, and every evil assignment. Your Word declares that we overcome by the blood of the Lamb, and I decree that the blood speaks peace, safety, and restoration over this household.

Father, fill this home with love, joy, laughter, and healing. Let worship rise here. Let praise shift the atmosphere. Your Word says You inhabit the praises of Your people (Psalm 22:3), and I declare that as praise fills this home, fear must leave. I decree that this house is a sanctuary—a place of rest, renewal, and refuge.

I declare that fear has no place in this home, for "The LORD is my light and my salvation; whom shall I fear? The LORD is the strength of my life; of whom shall I be afraid?" (Psalm 27:1). I speak peace in the night, peace in conversations, peace in relationships, and peace in rest. This home is governed by faith, covered by grace, and protected by Your presence.

I seal this prayer by faith, declaring that my home is blessed, protected, and filled with the peace of God. In the mighty name of Jesus Christ, Amen.

Prayer For The Salvation Of Loved Ones

Father God, I come before You in the authority of Jesus Christ, standing on Your Word and trusting Your heart for those I love. I lift before You my loved ones by name—those You have placed in my care and in my prayers. You desire that none should perish but that all should come to repentance (2 Peter 3:9), and I align my faith with Your will for their salvation.

Father, I ask for divine intervention in their lives. Wherever blindness, confusion, pride, fear, or deception has clouded their understanding, I ask that You remove the veil. Your Word declares that the god of this world blinds the minds of unbelievers, but You shine light into darkness (2 Corinthians 4:4–6). Let the light of Christ break through every shadow and reveal truth with clarity and love.

In the name of Jesus Christ, I take authority over every spiritual obstacle standing in the way of their salvation. I bind and break the power of addiction, fear, rebellion, bondage, shame, and destructive patterns that have kept them distant from You. I renounce and sever every generational curse—every bloodline pattern of rejection, addiction, unbelief, anger, poverty, or confusion—by the blood of Jesus. Your Word declares that whom the Son sets free is free indeed (John 8:36), and I decree freedom over their lives now.

Father, I plead the blood of Jesus over my loved ones. Let the blood speak mercy, redemption, and deliverance. Let it cleanse their hearts, quiet their minds, and dismantle every legal ground the enemy has used against them. I declare that the blood of Jesus cancels every evil declaration, breaks every ungodly covenant, and opens the way for repentance and restoration.

Holy Spirit, I invite You to move powerfully in their hearts. Convict with love, not condemnation. Draw them with cords of kindness and truth. Your Word says that no one can come to Jesus unless the Father draws them (John 6:44), and I ask You now to draw them—through dreams, encounters, conversations, and divine interruptions. Let their hearts become soft, receptive, and responsive to Your voice.

Father, where fear has kept them bound, release peace. Where trauma has hardened their hearts, bring healing. Where pride has resisted surrender, release humility. I ask that You replace every counterfeit comfort with Your presence, and every false refuge with the peace that only You can give. Let them encounter You not as religion, but as a living, loving Savior.

I declare that salvation is coming to my household. Your Word says, "Believe in the Lord Jesus, and you will be saved—you and your household" (Acts 16:31). I stand on that promise. I declare that my loved ones will know You, love You, and walk in truth. Their steps are being redirected. Their hearts are being awakened. Their destiny is being aligned with heaven.

Father, I thank You in advance for the testimonies that will come from their transformation. I trust You with the timing, the process, and the outcome. What You have begun, You will complete.

I seal this prayer in faith, believing that the Holy Spirit is moving even now. In the mighty, saving, delivering name of Jesus Christ, Amen.

SECTION IV — ADVANCED WARFARE PRAYERS

Some battles break only through alignment with Heaven's authority

As discernment deepens, prayer becomes more precise. This section addresses deeper layers of spiritual resistance, requiring humility, alignment, and dependence on God's authority. These prayers are not about spiritual bravado, but about standing in Christ while inviting God to dismantle what opposes His will.

Prayer For Deliverance From Spiritual Spouses & Night Attacks

Father God, I come before You in the supreme authority of Jesus Christ, seated with Him in heavenly places, far above all principality, power, ruler of darkness, and spiritual wickedness. I do not come in my own strength—I come clothed in the victory of the cross and armed with the Word of God.

In the name of Jesus Christ, I confront and expose every spiritual spouse, spirit husband, spirit wife, incubus, succubus, and every demonic personality operating through dreams, night visits, soul ties, or counterfeit intimacy. I declare that you are illegal in my life. You were never authorized by God, and your access ends now.

By the authority of Jesus Christ, I renounce and reject every conscious or unconscious covenant, vow, agreement, or consent made with any spiritual spouse—whether through dreams, trauma, ancestral altars, idolatry, lust, abuse, or generational sin. I renounce every ancestral marriage, bloodline covenant, dedication, or sacrifice that opened doors to these spirits. I reject them completely—spirit, soul, and body.

I decree a DIVORCE BY FIRE from every spiritual marriage now.

I nullify every demonic contract.

I cancel every spiritual union.

I revoke every claim, right, and access point.

According to Isaiah 54:17, no weapon formed against me shall prosper—and every tongue that rises in judgment is condemned. I declare that every spiritual ring, garment, mark, or seal placed upon me by these spirits is removed and destroyed by the fire of the Holy Ghost.

I plead the Blood of Jesus over my body, my soul, my spirit, my dreams, my sleep, and my subconscious. Let the blood of Jesus erase every imprint, cleanse every defilement, and silence every voice speaking in the night. I declare that the blood speaks better things than any covenant made in darkness (Hebrews 12:24).

In the name of Jesus, I break every cord, soul tie, and spiritual attachment binding me to these entities. I cut them now—by fire, by the Word, and by the blood of Jesus. Every cord feeding these spirits is severed. Every channel of access is closed permanently.

I address every night attack—sexual dreams, paralysis, fear, draining, monitoring, manipulation, and spiritual harassment. I declare that my sleep is redeemed. My rest is sanctified. My night seasons belong to the Lord. According to Psalm 4:8, I will lie down and sleep in peace, for You alone, Lord, make me dwell in safety.

Father, release angelic protection around me now. Let warrior angels stand guard over my bed, my room, my home, and my atmosphere. I declare that my dwelling is filled with the presence of God, and every intruder is expelled by holy fire.

I reclaim my authority. I reclaim my body. I reclaim my identity.

I declare out loud and in the spirit realm:

My covenant is with Christ.

My body is the temple of the Holy Spirit.

I belong wholly and eternally to the Lord.

I declare that every spiritual spouse is permanently expelled, bound, and forbidden from returning. I seal every gate—dream gates, soul gates, and spiritual gates—with the blood of Jesus. I declare total freedom, restoration, and peace.

Holy Spirit, fill every place that was violated. Where darkness operated, bring light. Where corruption entered, bring holiness. Where fear existed, establish peace. I receive healing, wholeness, and divine order.

I seal this deliverance by faith. What You set free is free indeed.

I stand restored, protected, and victorious. In the mighty, all-conquering name of Jesus Christ, Amen.

Declarations — Breaking Altars That Feed Spirit Spouses

Declaration 1 — Ancestral Altars

In the name of Jesus Christ, I come against every **ancestral altar** operating in my bloodline that has fed spiritual spouses, night attacks, or counterfeit covenants. By the blood of Jesus, I disconnect from every sacrifice, vow, or dedication made on my behalf. I declare that the influence of these altars is broken, their voice is silenced, and their power is permanently destroyed.

Declaration 2 — Household Altars

I declare that every **household altar**—known or unknown—raising itself against my purity, peace, identity, or destiny is dismantled now. I renounce every open door created through sin, trauma, ignorance, or inheritance. I decree that my household belongs to the Lord, and no altar has authority to operate within my life or lineage.

Declaration 3 — Marine Altars

By the authority of Jesus Christ, I confront every **marine altar** fueling spirit spouses, dream manipulation, night visitation, or spiritual pollution. I declare that these altars are cut off from my life. Every spiritual supply line feeding from them is severed by the blood of Jesus, and their influence over my body, sleep, and destiny is ended permanently.

Declaration 4 — Evil Shrines & Hidden Structures

I address every **evil shrine, hidden altar, or demonic structure**—whether erected knowingly or unknowingly—speaking against my life. I declare that the fire of God consumes their foundation, and the blood of Jesus erases every legal record connected to them. They no longer speak, function, or demand anything from me.

Declaration 5 — Covenant Termination

I declare that every altar-based covenant, spiritual marriage, or demonic agreement is terminated now. According to Hebrews 12:24, the blood of Jesus speaks better things over my life than any sacrifice made in darkness. I choose covenant with Christ alone.

Declaration 6 — Restoration & Authority

I reclaim my spiritual authority, purity, and inheritance. What was taken through altars is restored. What was delayed is released. What was bound is now free. I declare that my life is aligned with the altar of the Lord, and no counterfeit altar will ever rise again.

Declaration 7 — Sealing

I seal these declarations by the blood of Jesus. Every altar broken remains broken. Every door closed remains closed. I stand delivered, protected, and restored in Christ.

In the name of Jesus Christ, Amen.

Prayer Against Monitoring Spirits & Demonic Surveillance

Father God, I come before You in the authority of Jesus Christ, standing on the victory of the cross and the power of Your Word. I declare that my life is hidden with Christ in God, and no force of darkness has permission to watch, track, interfere, or report on what You are doing in me or through me.

In the name of Jesus Christ, I confront and silence every monitoring spirit, familiar spirit, demonic observer, and spiritual surveillance assigned to study my movements, delay my progress, or interfere with my destiny. I declare that your access is revoked. Your sight is cut off. Your assignments are terminated now by the authority of Jesus Christ.

Father, let Your consuming fire go before me and dismantle every system of darkness monitoring my life. Your Word declares, "The LORD thy God is he which goeth over before thee; as a consuming fire he shall destroy them" (Deuteronomy 9:3). I decree that the fire of God consumes every spiritual lens, mirror, altar, and platform used to gather information against me. Let every evil network tracking my steps be burned, scattered, and destroyed.

I plead the blood of Jesus over my life—over my past, my present, my future, my plans, my dreams, and my progress. Let the blood of Jesus erase every spiritual footprint used against me. Let it silence every accusation, cancel every report, and cleanse every access point the enemy has used. Your Word declares that Jesus "spoiled principalities and powers, [and] made a shew of them openly, triumphing over them in it" (Colossians 2:15). I declare that the victory of the cross speaks freedom, authority, and protection over me now.

In the name of Jesus, I seal every gate of access—dream gates, soul gates, spiritual gates, and generational entry points. I declare that what God has closed, no one can open, and what God has sealed, no power can breach. I decree divine restriction against every unauthorized spirit attempting to re-enter my life.

Father, release confusion into the camp of the enemy. As You did for the enemies of Your people, let their plans turn against them. Let every assignment collapse under its own weight. Your Word says, "He disappointeth the devices of the crafty, so that their hands cannot perform their enterprise" (Job 5:12). I declare that every strategy formed against me fails now.

Holy Spirit, fill every space that darkness attempted to occupy. Where observation tried to limit me, bring freedom. Where interference tried to delay me, release acceleration. Where intimidation tried to silence me, release boldness. I declare that I move forward unhindered, uncovered by darkness, and unrestricted by spiritual opposition.

Father, surround me with Your presence as a shield and a guard. Your Word declares, "The LORD shall preserve thee from all evil: he shall preserve thy soul" (Psalm 121:7). I declare that my life is protected, my progress is preserved, and my destiny is secure in You.

I stand in victory. I walk in freedom. I move forward with clarity and authority.

Every eye watching me illegally is blinded.

Every voice speaking against me is silenced.

Every assignment formed against my life is canceled.

I seal this prayer by faith, knowing that what You secure, no enemy can breach. In the mighty, victorious name of Jesus Christ, Amen.

Prayer To Dismantle Strongholds & High Places

Father God, I come before You in the authority of Jesus Christ, standing on the finished work of the cross and the power of Your Word. I acknowledge that the weapons of my warfare are not carnal, but mighty through God for pulling down strongholds (2 Corinthians 10:4). I do not fight with human strength or reasoning—I fight with divine authority.

In the name of Jesus Christ, I confront every stronghold, every fortified lie, every pattern of thinking, and every spiritual structure that has exalted itself against the knowledge of God in my life. I address high places of pride, fear, trauma, unbelief, shame, addiction, confusion, rebellion, and control. I command you now—come down. You will not remain standing.

According to the Word of God, "Casting down imaginations, and every high thing that exalteth itself against the knowledge of God, and bringing into captivity every thought to the obedience of Christ" (2 Corinthians 10:5), I pull down every imagination, argument, and mental barrier that has resisted truth. I declare that my mind belongs to Christ. Every thought aligns with truth. Every lie loses its power.

In the name of Jesus, I dismantle every spiritual high place erected through trauma, generational patterns, false teaching, idolatry, fear, or repeated sin. Your Word declares that the Lord alone will be exalted, and every high place will be brought low (Isaiah 2:11–12). I decree that no structure raised against God's authority in my life will remain.

I plead the blood of Jesus over my mind, my emotions, my memories, and my identity. Let the blood cleanse every place where deception took root. Let it erase every legal claim the enemy has used to reinforce these strongholds. I declare that where sin once strengthened bondage, grace now establishes freedom.

Father, let the fire of the Holy Spirit fall and consume every remaining residue of darkness. Burn away stubborn patterns. Destroy cycles that refused to break. Reduce fortified lies to ashes. I declare that every altar feeding these strongholds is destroyed, and every supply line sustaining them is cut off now.

Holy Spirit, replace what has been torn down with truth. Where lies ruled, establish revelation. Where fear dominated, release peace. Where confusion lingered, bring clarity. Where oppression pressed in, release liberty. Your Word declares, "Where the Spirit of the Lord is, there is liberty" (2 Corinthians 3:17), and I receive that liberty now.

I declare that my life is aligned with the truth of God. I walk with a renewed mind, a guarded heart, and a Spirit-led life. No stronghold will rebuild. No high place will rise again. My foundation is Christ, and my life is established on truth.

I seal this prayer by faith, declaring that what has been pulled down remains dismantled, and what God has established will stand. In the mighty, victorious name of Jesus Christ, Amen.

Prayer For God's Authority Over Territorial Opposition

Father God, I come before You humbly and boldly through Jesus Christ, who has been given all authority in heaven and on earth. I acknowledge that You alone are sovereign, and that every power, principality, and authority answers to You. I do not rely on my own strength or position, but I stand in submission to Your rule and Your Kingdom.

Your Word declares that Christ is seated far above all principality, power, might, and dominion, and every name that is named, not only in this world, but also in that which is to come (Ephesians 1:21), and that all things are under His feet. I align myself with that truth now. I ask that You establish the authority of Christ fully in every area where I live, move, work, and worship.

Father, I ask You to dismantle anything operating in opposition to Your will and Your Kingdom in the regions and environments connected to my life. Where unseen powers have sought to influence atmospheres through fear, confusion, violence, corruption, deception, or resistance to truth, I ask You to remove their influence and render their efforts ineffective. Let Your Kingdom come, and let Your will be done on earth as it is in heaven.

Lord, Your Word teaches me that though I walk in the flesh, I do not wage war according to the flesh. The weapons of my warfare are not carnal, but mighty through God for pulling down strongholds (2 Corinthians 10:3–4). I stand firm—watchful, sober, and steadfast in faith—resisting every attempt of the enemy to intimidate or distract me (1 Peter 5:8–9). Strengthen me to stand without fear, distraction, or compromise.

Father, I ask You to confuse and overturn every scheme designed to hinder Your purposes for my life, my family, and my future. Your Word declares that You bring the counsel of the nations to nothing and make the plans of the peoples of no effect (Psalm 33:10). Let every plan that does not originate from You fail before it takes root.

I ask You to release Your angelic protection according to Your will. Your Word declares, "Are they not all ministering spirits, sent forth to minister for them who shall be heirs of salvation?" (Hebrews 1:14). Let them guard my home, my steps, my family, and every assignment You have entrusted to me.

Father, I declare that I am surrounded by You as the mountains surround Jerusalem, both now and forevermore (Psalm 125:2). Evil will not prevail against what You have established, and nothing operates outside of Your authority. I trust You as my defender, my refuge, and my strong tower.

Holy Spirit, guide me in discernment and obedience. Alert me to what I need to pray, when I need to stand, and where I need to remain still. Teach me to partner with heaven through humility, faith, and trust rather than fear.

I rest in this truth: the battle belongs to the Lord (2 Chronicles 20:15). I stand firm, confident that You are working even where I cannot see, ruling over all things for Your glory and my good.

I seal this prayer in faith, submitting fully to Your authority and trusting in Your power. In the mighty and matchless name of Jesus Christ, Amen

Prayer To Break Soul Ties (Old, Toxic, or Unhealthy)

Father God, I come before You in humility and truth, submitting myself fully to Your authority and to the lordship of Jesus Christ. I acknowledge that You alone are the healer and restorer of my soul. I ask You now to search my heart and reveal every connection, attachment, or bond that was formed outside of Your will and has brought harm, confusion, or spiritual compromise into my life.

Father, I repent for every unhealthy attachment I entered into knowingly or unknowingly. I repent for every relationship I made an idol—through emotional dependence, sexual sin, misplaced loyalty, or any bond that drew my heart away from You. I renounce every soul tie formed through sin, manipulation, control, trauma, fear, or counterfeit intimacy. Your Word warns me to keep myself from idols (1 John 5:21), and I obey that command now. I turn my heart fully back to You, and I surrender every affection, connection, and attachment that competed with Your place in my life.

In the name of Jesus Christ, by the power of His blood, I declare that every ungodly soul tie connected to my past—every toxic relationship, former partner, emotional bond, or spiritual attachment that You did not ordain—is severed now. I cut every cord, every chain, and every tie that connects my soul to anything that is not aligned with Your will. What You did not join together, I declare broken by the authority of Jesus' name.

I command every unclean spirit, every spirit of control, lust, perversion, manipulation, fear, rejection, heaviness, or confusion that entered my life through these relationships to leave now. You have no legal right to remain. I resist you, and I stand on the promise that when I submit to God, the enemy must flee (James 4:7). I declare that my soul belongs to the Lord, and no other voice, influence, or attachment has power over me.

Father, cleanse my soul now by the blood of Jesus. Where pieces of my heart were fragmented, reclaim them. Where my emotions were entangled, bring order. Where my mind was affected, restore clarity and peace. Your Word says You restore my soul (Psalm 23:3), and I receive that restoration fully—emotionally, mentally, and spiritually.

Holy Spirit, fill every place where a soul tie has been broken. Heal the wounds left behind. Rebuild my identity in truth. Teach me to love from wholeness, not from need. Lead me into relationships that honor You and produce life, peace, and freedom. Guard my heart moving forward, and align my desires with Your perfect will.

I declare that I am free. I am whole. I am restored. My soul is anchored in Christ alone.

I seal this prayer in faith, by the blood of Jesus, and I walk forward healed and delivered.

In the mighty and liberating name of Jesus Christ, Amen

SECTION VI — PRAYERS TO STRENGTHEN YOUR WALK

Strong warfare flows from a strong walk with God.

Victory must be sustained. This section focuses on spiritual growth, maturity, intimacy with God, and hearing His voice clearly. Strong warfare flows from a strong walk.

Prayer For Spiritual Growth & Maturity

Father God, I come before You with a hunger to grow. I do not want to remain where I am spiritually, and I refuse to settle for immaturity when You have called me to fullness in Christ. Draw me deeper into relationship with You. Teach me how to walk in the Spirit, not led by impulse, emotion, or flesh, but by truth and obedience. I desire to know You—not just what You can do, but who You are.

Your Word says that those who hunger and thirst for righteousness shall be filled (Matthew 5:6). I bring that hunger to You now. Shape my desires so they align with Yours. Where I have tolerated compromise, correct me. Where I have excused sin, convict me. Give me a heart that hates what You hate and loves what You love. Let holiness become my pursuit, not out of obligation, but out of love for You.

Lord, I ask for wisdom and understanding as I open Your Word. Your Word declares that if anyone lacks wisdom, You give generously without reproach (James 1:5). Open my eyes to see truth clearly. Train me to rightly divide Scripture, not for knowledge alone, but for transformation. Let Your Word take root in me, producing discernment, endurance, and spiritual depth.

Father, I renounce spiritual laziness and immaturity. I turn away from habits that dull my sensitivity to Your voice. Strengthen me to overcome temptation, not through willpower, but through dependence on Your grace. Teach me to submit my thoughts, my actions, and my desires to You daily. Let my life reflect steady growth, not emotional cycles.

Your Word says that maturity comes through practice—by those who have trained their senses to discern good and evil (Hebrews 5:14). Train me, Lord. Discipline me in love. Grow me in patience, humility, and obedience. Let my faith become rooted and unshakable, not tossed by circumstance or opinion.

Holy Spirit, guide me into truth. Correct me when I drift. Warn me when I am close to compromise. Empower me to live a life that honors God even when no one else is watching. I ask for grace to walk uprightly, to choose truth over convenience, and obedience over comfort.

I declare that I am growing in Christ. I am maturing in faith. I am being transformed by the renewing of my mind. My walk with God is deepening, my discernment is sharpening, and my life is bearing fruit that glorifies You.

I commit myself to this journey of growth—not in my own strength, but abiding in You. Finish the work You have begun in me. In the name of Jesus Christ, Amen.

Prayer For Hearing God's Voice Clearly

Father God, I come before You with a desire to hear You clearly. I quiet my heart before You now, laying down every distraction, every competing voice, and every noise that has crowded my spirit. Your Word says that You are not the author of confusion, but of peace, and I ask You to establish that peace within me so I may discern Your voice without interference.

Your Word declares that You speak in a still, small voice (1 Kings 19:12), and I ask You to tune my heart to recognize it. Remove every spiritual blockage that dulls my sensitivity; fear, anxiety, unbelief, distraction, and past wounds that make me hesitate to trust what You say. Cleanse my spiritual ears and sharpen my discernment by Your Spirit.

Holy Spirit, I invite You to lead me. Your Word says that those who are led by the Spirit of God are the children of God (Romans 8:14). Teach me to recognize Your prompting, Your correction, and Your guidance. Train me to discern the difference between my own thoughts, the voices of the world, and Your truth.

Father, silence every voice that is not from You. I resist confusion, deception, and distraction. I reject fear-based thinking and emotional noise that clouds my judgment. I ask You to still my soul, as Your Word says You guide the humble in what is right and teach them Your way (Psalm 25:9).

Give me a heart that listens and a spirit that obeys. Your Word declares, "My sheep hear My voice, and I know them, and they follow Me" (John 10:27). I receive that promise now. I declare that I hear Your voice clearly, consistently, and confidently. I recognize truth. I respond with obedience.

Holy Spirit, correct me when I am off course. Warn me when I am about to make decisions outside of Your will. Guide me in moments of uncertainty. Speak to me through Your Word, through prayer, and through peace that confirms Your direction.

I surrender my will to Yours. I choose sensitivity over stubbornness, obedience over impulse, and trust over fear. I thank You that You are speaking, and that I am learning to listen.

I declare that my spiritual ears are open, my heart is aligned, and my spirit is attentive. I walk forward led by God, guided by truth, and anchored in peace.

In the name of Jesus Christ, Amen.

Prayer For Wisdom, Strategy & Divine Instruction

Father God, I come before You acknowledging that true wisdom comes from You alone. Your Word declares that if anyone lacks wisdom, they should ask You, who gives generously and without reproach (James 1:5). I ask You now for wisdom that is pure, peaceable, discerning, and led by Your Spirit.

Holy Spirit, I invite You into every decision before me. Where there has been confusion, bring clarity. Where there has been hesitation, bring confidence rooted in truth. I reject haste, pressure, and fear-driven choices. I choose to wait on Your instruction and move only at Your direction.

Father, release divine strategy into my life. Give me insight beyond natural understanding. Show me the hidden keys that unlock progress, favor, and breakthrough. Your Word says You reveal deep and hidden things and know what lies in darkness, and light dwells with You (Daniel 2:22). I receive revelation that exposes the right path and protects me from unseen traps.

Holy Spirit, grant me wisdom for conversations, meetings, and decisions. Put the right words in my mouth at the right time. Let my speech be seasoned with grace and guided by truth. Give me understanding not only of what to do, but when to do it and how to do it well.

Father, I ask You to release creative insight and divine ideas. Your Word declares that it is You who gives the ability to create and produce (Exodus 35:31–32). I receive witty inventions, innovative solutions, and fresh ideas inspired by Your Spirit—ideas that bring progress, excellence, and impact.

Guard me from deception and misalignment. Holy Spirit, alert me when something looks right but is not from You. Lead me away from the snares of the enemy and into paths of wisdom and peace. Your Word says You will instruct me and teach me in the way I should go; You will guide me with Your eye (Psalm 32:8).

I declare that I am led, not lost. I walk with clarity, not confusion. I move with strategy, not struggle. My steps are ordered by the Lord, and His wisdom establishes my path.

Thank You, Father, that You do not withhold instruction from those who seek You. I trust You to lead me wisely, guide me faithfully, and establish every step I take.

In the name of Jesus Christ, Amen.

Prayer For God's Presence, Power & Fresh Fire

Father God, I come before You with hunger in my spirit and surrender in my heart. I do not ask for power apart from Your presence, nor fire apart from holiness. I ask for You—to dwell with me, fill me, and consume every place where my love has grown dim or distracted.

Holy Spirit, I ask for a fresh baptism of fire. Not yesterday's oil, not borrowed passion—but fresh filling for this season. Your Word declares that You baptize with the Holy Spirit and with fire (Matthew 3:11). Ignite my spirit again. Burn away complacency, compromise, and spiritual fatigue. Let what is not from You be consumed, and let what is from You be strengthened.

Father, I yield my life fully to You. I declare, "It is no longer I who live, but Christ who lives in me" (Galatians 2:20). Let my thoughts reflect Christ. Let my words carry Christ. Let my life reveal Christ. Teach me to walk in holiness—not out of fear, but out of love and reverence for You.

Clothe me with divine strength and spiritual authority. Your Word says You train my hands for battle and my fingers for war (Psalm 144:1). Teach me how to stand, how to resist, how to pray, and how to overcome—by the power of Your Spirit, not by flesh or emotion. Make me discerning, watchful, and grounded in truth.

Holy Spirit, fill me until Your fruit overflows—love, joy, peace, patience, kindness, goodness, faithfulness, gentleness, and self-control (Galatians 5:22–23). Let my fire be pure, my zeal be steady, and my walk be mature. Keep me burning without burning out.

Father, release divine energy and spiritual refreshing into my soul. Restore what has been drained. Renew what has been weary. Strengthen me in my inner being with power through Your Spirit (Ephesians 3:16). Let Your presence become my refuge, my confidence, and my sustaining force.

I ask You to make me a vessel of light in dark places. Let Your fire within me illuminate truth, expose deception, and draw others to You—not through noise, but through presence and power. Establish me as one who carries Your glory with humility and obedience.

I declare that I will not grow cold, distracted, or dormant. I will remain fervent in spirit, serving the Lord (Romans 12:11). I welcome Your intervention, Your refining, and Your leading.

Come and dwell with me, Lord.

Come and fill me again.

Come and ignite fresh fire within me.

In the mighty and holy name of Jesus Christ, Amen.

SECTION VII — DECLARATIONS & DAILY WARFARE CONFESSIONS

What you speak daily determines what you sustain spiritually.

This section equips you with declarations to reinforce truth, guard identity, and maintain spiritual posture daily. Here, warfare becomes a lifestyle of alignment, not a reaction to crisis.

Daily Decrees Of Victory

These decrees are spoken aloud in faith and agreement with Heaven. They are not emotional affirmations—they are spiritual alignments with the authority of Jesus Christ and the finished work of the cross.

Today, I decree that Jesus Christ is Lord over my life.

My spirit, soul, and body are submitted to Him. I renounce fear, delay, and compromise, and I align myself fully with the will of God.

I decree that every evil agenda formed against my life is exposed and dismantled.

Every hidden plan, demonic assignment, and strategy working behind the scenes is overturned by the power of God. No scheme will mature, advance, or prevail.

By the blood of Jesus, I secure every blessing assigned to my life.

Nothing meant for my destruction will follow me, and nothing meant for my blessing will pass me by. I recover what was delayed, stolen, or withheld.

I decree that I walk in faith and not in fear.

Fear has no authority over my decisions, my future, or my destiny. My trust is in the Lord, and my confidence is anchored in His promises.

I decree divine restoration over every area of my life.

What was broken is healed. What was lost is restored. What was delayed is accelerated by the hand of God.

I decree acceleration and forward movement.

Every cycle of stagnation, delay, and limitation is broken. I move in divine timing, divine order, and divine momentum.

I decree that I walk under unconditional favor.

Doors open that no one can shut. Help comes from unexpected places. I am favored by God and positioned for His purposes.

I decree that my mind is guarded by peace and truth.

Confusion, anxiety, intimidation, and heaviness are dismissed. I think clearly, discern accurately, and respond wisely.

I decree that my steps are ordered by the Lord.

I will not miss divine opportunities or walk into traps. The Holy Spirit directs my choices and establishes my path.

By the blood of Jesus, I decree divine protection.

My life, my household, my assignments, and my future are covered. Every curse is broken. Every evil agreement is canceled. Every open door to darkness is sealed.

I decree that I overcome by the blood of the Lamb and the word of my testimony.

I am not defeated, confused, or powerless. I stand in victory because Christ has already won.

Today, I choose faith over fear.

Truth over deception.

Light over darkness.

Obedience over compromise.

I walk boldly, covered by the blood, strengthened by the Spirit, and aligned with Heaven. So it is. In Jesus' mighty name, Amen.

Declarations For Identity & Authority

I declare that my identity is rooted in Christ alone.

I am no longer a slave to fear, sin, or condemnation. I have been transferred out of darkness and into the Kingdom of God's dear Son.

I declare that I walk in the position God has assigned to me.

I am not chasing influence—I am led by the Spirit. I do not follow confusion, failure, or delay. I move in divine order and authority.

I declare that the authority I carry flows from my submission to Christ.

I do not operate in my own strength, but in the power of the Holy Spirit. Because I submit to God, I can resist the enemy, and he must flee.

I declare that I operate from Heaven's perspective.

I am seated with Christ, not reacting to circumstances but responding through wisdom, prayer, and obedience.

I declare that my mind is renewed by truth.

Every lie, accusation, and false identity spoken against me is silenced. I receive the mind of Christ and walk in discernment and wisdom.

I declare that I am clothed in spiritual authority.

I walk in humility, obedience, and confidence. Darkness recognizes the name of Jesus, and I stand in His victory.

I declare that I have been given authority to overcome.

Not by force, not by fear, but by faith in the finished work of Christ. I overcome through obedience, endurance, and alignment with God's Word.

I declare that my voice carries weight in the spirit because my life is aligned with Heaven.

My prayers are effective, my declarations are rooted in truth, and my steps are ordered by the Lord.

I declare that I am seated with Christ in heavenly places.

I do not live beneath pressure, intimidation, or spiritual oppression. I live from a place of victory, rest, and authority in Him.

I declare that I walk in freedom and dominion.

Every chain is broken. Every false limitation is removed. I am free to obey God fully and walk boldly in my calling.

I declare that my authority is guarded by humility and obedience.

I do not operate in pride or presumption. I listen to the Holy Spirit, submit to God's will, and move when He leads.

I am who God says I am.

I have what He says I have.

I can do what He has called me to do.

I walk in identity. I stand in authority. I live under the Lordship of Jesus Christ. In Jesus' name, Amen.

Declarations For Protection & Peace

I declare that I dwell under the covering of the Most High God.

I abide under the shadow of the Almighty, and no evil shall overtake me. The Lord is my refuge, my fortress, and my defender.

I plead and apply the Blood of Jesus over my life, my home, my family, and my health.

The Blood speaks better things—protection, deliverance, healing, and victory. Every accusation, assignment, and threat is silenced by the Blood of Jesus.

I declare divine immunity in Christ Jesus.

No weapon formed against me shall prosper. No plague, disaster, or scheme of darkness is permitted to breach what God has covered.

I declare that my home is a sanctuary of peace and holiness.

The presence of God fills every room. The fire of the Holy Spirit surrounds my dwelling as a wall of protection. Every spirit of strife, fear, confusion, and unrest is driven out now.

I declare angelic protection released by the command of the Lord.

God's angels encamp around me and my household. They guard our coming and going, secure our steps, and protect every assignment God has entrusted to us.

I declare peace over my mind, my emotions, and my body.

Fear has no authority here. Anxiety has no voice. I receive the peace of God that surpasses understanding, guarding my heart and my mind in Christ Jesus.

I declare that every spiritual chain and assignment of darkness is broken.

Curses, affliction, generational patterns, and cycles of unrest are dismantled by the power of the Holy Spirit. I walk in freedom, rest, and divine order.

I declare protection over my family and loved ones.

They are hidden in Christ. They are covered by the Blood. No plan of the enemy shall prevail against their lives, destinies, or peace.

I declare that my body is a temple of the Holy Spirit.

Sickness, disease, and infirmity have no legal right. I receive healing, strength, and wholeness through the life of Christ within me.

I declare that I live fearless, anchored in faith.

I am not moved by reports, threats, or circumstances. I am governed by the Word of God and the leading of the Holy Spirit.

I declare that peace rules my life.

The Prince of Peace reigns over my heart, my home, and my future. I rest in God's protection, confident in His power and faithful care.

I walk covered.

I walk protected.

I walk in peace.

In the mighty name of Jesus, Amen.

Declarations For Breakthrough & Blessing

I declare that this is my appointed season of breakthrough.

Every delay is broken, every barrier is removed, and every door God has ordained for my life is opening now by His power.

I declare divine acceleration in every area of my life.

What was held up is released. What was resisted is moving. What was stalled is advancing according to God's perfect timing.

I declare that the hand of the Lord is upon me for favor and increase.

I walk into opportunities I did not create, access I did not earn, and blessings I did not manipulate. God is doing what only He can do.

I declare that every evil agenda working against my progress is overturned.

Hidden opposition is exposed. Spiritual resistance is dismantled. Every plan not planted by God is uprooted and rendered powerless.

I declare that the Blood of Jesus speaks blessing, restoration, and victory over my life.

Every loss is redeemed. Every setback is reversed. What the enemy meant for harm, God is turning for my good.

I declare open doors that no man can shut.

Doors of provision, purpose, clarity, promotion, and destiny are unlocked by the Lord Himself. I step boldly into what God has prepared for me.

I declare supernatural provision and sufficiency.

I will not lack. I will not live in fear of shortage. My God supplies all my needs according to His riches in glory through Christ Jesus.

I declare restoration of time, resources, and opportunities.

Years that were wasted, stolen, or attacked are being redeemed. God is restoring what was lost and rebuilding what was broken.

I declare that my obedience positions me for blessing.

As I walk in alignment with God's Word, blessings pursue me, overtake me, and establish me firmly in His will.

I declare that I am the head and not the tail.

I am above and not beneath. I advance, I overcome, and I prosper in the assignment God has given me.

I declare faith over fear and expectation over doubt.

I do not shrink back. I do not settle. I move forward trusting God to perform what He has promised.

I declare that my life produces visible fruit.

Breakthrough is not temporary—it is sustained. Blessing is not accidental—it is established by the Lord.

I walk in breakthrough.

I live under blessing.

I move forward by faith.

In the powerful name of Jesus, Amen.

Final Exhortation

You have not prayed these prayers in vain, nor have you spoken these declarations as mere words. What has been established here is not emotional momentum, but spiritual alignment. You have positioned yourself under the Lordship of Jesus Christ, clothed in truth, anchored in obedience, and strengthened by the Spirit of God.

This book was not written to produce believers who strive, but those who stand firmly in Christ. Not those who chase power, but those who walk in authority rooted in intimacy with God. What you carry now is not self-derived confidence—it is the fruit of submission, truth, and agreement with Heaven.

As you go forward, remember this: spiritual authority is sustained by spiritual maturity. Victory is preserved through obedience, and breakthrough is guarded by humility. Walk closely with the Lord. Remain sensitive to the Holy Spirit. Stay anchored in the Word. Let prayer be your posture, not your last resort. Do not measure your authority by how loud you speak, but by how faithfully you obey. Walk in the light so consistently that darkness cannot remain. Let your life testify before your words ever do.

You are not sent out fearful or uncertain. You are sent out established. You are not fighting for victory—you are enforcing what Christ has already won. You are not operating alone—He goes before you, surrounds you, and lives within you.

Stand firm. Walk holy. Pray boldly. Speak truth. Love deeply. Resist the enemy. Submit to God. Trust the Lord with what is beyond your reach, and obey Him in what He places within your hands.

May your life reflect the Kingdom of God.

May your steps be ordered.

May your discernment be sharp.

May your heart remain pure.

May your authority remain guarded by humility.

May your faith remain unshaken.

You are who God says you are.

You carry what He has entrusted to you.

You walk forward under His covering, by His Spirit, for His glory.

Go in peace.

Stand in authority.

Live submitted.

In Jesus' name, Amen.

A Final Word On Transformation & Responsibility

Applied Behavior Analysis, often referred to as ABA, is a therapeutic approach commonly used to help individuals understand, learn, and develop meaningful life skills by recognizing how behavior is shaped and changed over time. It focuses on identifying patterns, understanding why certain behaviors occur, and teaching healthier responses through consistent guidance, repetition, and reinforcement. At its heart, ABA is not about control—it is about support, growth, and helping a person move toward greater independence, stability, and quality of life.

When we look at Applied Behavior Analysis (ABA) therapy, we see a framework designed to understand how behavior is shaped. It observes three basic elements: what happens before a behavior (the antecedent), the behavior itself, and what happens after (the consequence). The goal is not punishment—it is growth. It is about identifying patterns, unlearning what is harmful, and replacing it with what leads to healthy functioning and wholeness.

When viewed through a biblical lens, this structure mirrors the way God lovingly engages with humanity. From the very beginning, God has been addressing not only individual choices, but patterns of behavior that flow through generations. Scripture repeatedly shows that what people practice, tolerate, and pass down becomes embedded in family lines, cultures, and nations. These inherited patterns function much like antecedents—conditions that shape how people respond to God, to themselves, and to others.

Many of the struggles we face did not originate with us. We inherited mindsets, coping mechanisms, fears, distortions, and survival behaviors from environments shaped by brokenness. These learned responses often made sense at one time—they protected, preserved or helped people endure hardship. But what once served as survival can later become a barrier to spiritual life "Do not conform to the pattern of this world, but be transformed by the renewing of your mind" (Romans 12:2).

God does not approach humanity with mere condemnation of behavior. He approaches with revelation and invitation "For God did not send his Son into the world to condemn the world, but to save the world through him" (John 3:17). Throughout Scripture, God exposes antecedents:

"You learned this."

"You were taught this."

"You have heard it said."

Then He introduces truth that challenges the old framework "You have heard that it was said... But I say to you..." (Matthew 5:21–22, 27–28, 33–34). This is not just correction, it is retraining "Teach me your way, O Lord, that I may walk in your truth" (Psalm 86:11). God is not simply trying to make people behave better. He is restoring people to their original design—to live in right relationship with Him.

Sin, at its core, is not only an act; it is a misalignment of relationship. It is humanity functioning under distorted beliefs about who God is, who we are, and how life works. Over time, these distortions produce predictable behaviors: fear, pride, control, rebellion, self-reliance, shame, and hiding "Your iniquities have separated you from your God" (Isaiah 59:2). God's redemptive work addresses the root, not just the symptom "You will know the truth, and the truth will set you free" (John 8:32).

He reveals truth (new antecedent).

He calls for repentance and faith (new response).

He releases grace, restoration, and transformation (new outcome).

This is spiritual reconditioning—not through force, but through love "Do you show contempt for the riches of his kindness, forbearance and patience, not realizing that God's kindness is intended to lead you to repentance?" (Romans 2:4)

Just as ABA therapy emphasizes consistency, patience, and reinforcement, God consistently presents His people with opportunities to choose a new way of living. He does not abandon us when we fall back into old patterns. He remains present, guiding, teaching, correcting, and strengthening "He who began a good work in you will carry it on to completion" (Philippians 1:6).

Salvation, then, is not merely a moment—it is the beginning of a lifelong process of learning to live in alignment with God's heart "Work out your own salvation with fear and trembling" (Philippians 2:12). God's true intention has always been relationship "I will be their God, and they will be my people" (Jeremiah 31:33).

Not behavior modification for appearance's sake.

Not external compliance.

But internal transformation.

"These people honor me with their lips, but their hearts are far from me." (Matthew 15:8)

He desires sons and daughters who know Him, trust Him, walk with Him, and reflect His nature. As we submit to His truth, the Holy Spirit begins to rewrite the internal scripts that once governed us. Old generational patterns lose authority. New patterns of righteousness, love, humility, and obedience take their place "For where the Spirit of the Lord is, there is freedom" (2 Corinthians 3:17).

What we are witnessing is not God controlling humanity.

We are witnessing God healing humanity.

He is restoring what was broken, re-training what was misaligned, and returning His people to the place they were always meant to live—in loving, surrendered, intimate relationship with Him "Return to me, and I will return to you" (Malachi 3:7).

The history of Israel vividly demonstrates how God engages with a people shaped by generational antecedents. Israel repeatedly inherited patterns of idolatry, unbelief, fear, and rebellion—often mirroring the nations around them. These behaviors did not emerge in isolation; they were learned, normalized, and passed down. Yet God continually sent prophets, judges, and leaders—not merely to announce punishment, but to call the people back into right relationship "Return, O Israel, to the Lord your God" (Hosea 14:1).

"You have forsaken the Lord."

"Return to the covenant."

"Choose this day whom you will serve."

Israel's story reveals a God who does not give up on His people. He patiently retrains a nation—generation after generation—toward covenant faithfulness. This same God now works in believers through Christ and the Holy Spirit, breaking old cycles and establishing new ones rooted in truth and love.

A Word of Encouragement

As you move forward, understand this: your life matters in the purposes of God. The choices you make, the truths you embrace, and the patterns you allow or reject shape not only your future, but the lives of those around you. God's work in you is deeply personal, but it is never isolated. You are being restored so that you can reflect Him in the world.

Transformation is not passive. It requires humility, repentance, and a willing heart. God reveals truth, but He also invites response. He exposes patterns, but He calls for alignment. Coming into right relationship with Him means agreeing with what He says about sin, righteousness, identity, and purpose—and choosing to live from that place.

You are not defined by what you inherited, what you survived, or what you have done. You are defined by who God says you are in Christ. As you submit to His truth, old identities lose their grip. New creation life takes root. You begin to live not from broken scripts, but from heaven's design.

God is forming you into a living witness of His grace, His authority, and His nature. Your obedience matters. Your surrender matters. Your growth matters. The world is impacted when believers walk in truth.

So take responsibility for your walk. Guard your heart. Renew your mind. Choose alignment daily. Not in your own strength—but through dependence on the Holy Spirit.

You are not merely being improved.

You are being restored.

You are not becoming someone new.

You are becoming who God always intended you to be.

About the Author

Donyae Jackson is an author with a passion for equipping believers to walk in the power, authority, and freedom found in Jesus Christ. Her passion for serving others flows from lived experience; real battles, real deliverance, and a deep reliance on the truth of God's Word.

Through her own journey with spiritual warfare, healing, and growth in discernment, Donyae has learned that victory is not achieved through self-effort, fear, or religious performance, but through intimacy with God, obedience to His Word, and alignment with the finished work of Christ. Donyae is committed to helping believers understand their identity in Christ, recognize spiritual opposition without becoming consumed by it, and develop a prayer life that flows from authority rather than desperation. Her work emphasizes spiritual maturity, discernment, and the importance of standing in truth while allowing God to confront what lies beyond human control.

Fire on the Altar, Authority in the Earth was written for those who desire a deeper walk with God; one marked by consistency, clarity, and confidence in Christ. Donyae's prayer is that readers would not only pray with power, but live from a place of surrendered authority, rooted in relationship with God and responsive to the leading of the Holy Spirit.

www.ingramcontent.com/pod-product-compliance
Lightning Source LLC
Chambersburg PA
CBHW051215160726
47994CB00002B/610